TOGETHER AS ONE

Legacy of James Shipley
World War II Tuskegee Airman

Jeremy P. Amick (signature)

Jeremy Paul Amick
©Copyright 2017

Cover Design by Jackie Polsgrove-Roberts

Cover Photo Credit: Jeremy Paul Amick

Published by:
Burnt District Press
Burnt District of Missouri, LLC
Harrisonville, Missouri 64701

Printed in the United States of America

TABLE OF CONTENTS

Acknowledgements

As is generally the case with any historical or literary endeavor, there are scores of individuals and organizations that have contributed through their knowledge, support or resources and deserve some form of recognition. First and foremost, I extend my eternal appreciation to James Shipley for the valuable time he provided and patience he demonstrated during the many interviews he endured over the course of the past several months. Secondly, I would like to extend my appreciation to the countless volunteers who have helped research the graves and burials that are listed on the *Find A Grave* website; your dedication to preserving this facet of our nation's history greatly assisted me in locating information regarding many of the airmen with whom Jim Shipley served. Also, for the dedication exemplified by the men of the 332nd Fighter Group, who, despite the obstacles placed before them, served their country with honor and dignity and have continued to share their heroic legacies with future generations. Finally, I must also recognize the members of the Shipley family who were so generous to provide me photographs, documents and stories related to Jim's life and service. Thank you, one and all.

Dedication

My darling wife, Tina, continues to instill in me the ceaseless inspiration to pursue ways to honor our nation's veterans. She has been a blessing to me and I look forward to our continued journey together. "Mit meiner ewigen Liebe, meine liebe Frau."

Foreword

There are several individuals who take immense pride in preserving and recording their family's history. After all, the recording of one's family history tends to represent a form of social importance. It also provides a microcosm of the context of the history through which that family has survived. However, this familial and historical representation for Black Americans has been very limited. The contributions of Black Americans in the historical records are relegated to a few accounts, which based on the measure of social importance would imply that they had not contributed much to society.

If written, the records of Black Americans are all-too-often only told of those that have reached some form of celebrity. This means that non-celebrities do not often get a chance to have their stories recorded and as a result, they do not hold a place within the history that they made. Therefore, a skewed representation has been provided to those that would attempt to understand history, how the everyday person was a part of it, and how those persons affected the historical events of their era. The story of James Shipley is no exception.

Until very recently, the name, James Shipley (my uncle), only provided a sense of recognition for those within our family and to those who had had the opportunity to get to know him. However, his story provides a glimpse into the lives and social constructs of the times in which he has lived. Born in rural Central Missouri just six years prior to the Great Depression's stock market crash of 1929, James Shipley was the middle son of a school teacher and a homemaker. Like all of the Blacks of Tipton, Missouri, James attended Harrison School, which was literally located on "the other side of the tracks." Harrison School was more than just a place of education, it was also of particular import for the Shipleys. James, his sister Geraldine, his brother David, and his youngest sister Rosalind all attended Harrison School together. Their studies were overseen by the Principal of Harrison School, Galveston Lee Roy Shipley (their father) and his father, Fred Shipley (the janitor).

Harrison School was relegated to function with used, hand-me-down materials and supplies that came from the White schools. However, James' father, Galveston Shipley, viewed education as a great social equalizer and led by example. Galveston took correspondence classes from Lincoln University and the University of Missouri from 1913 to 1949. He augmented his education for not only himself, but his students, as well. Through his interest in botany, Galveston Shipley developed a variety of peony flowers still seen around Tipton today.

When he was 19 years old, James Shipley, who had already dabbled as a mechanic in Tipton, voluntarily enlisted in the United States Army. After training in Alabama, he ultimately became a crew chief for the 332 Fighter Group, also known as the Tuskegee Airmen, the famous all-Black group that served in Italy during World War II. In that same year, his brother, David Shipley was drafted into the United States Navy without having completed high school. Both James and David served their country honorably, but they were placed within racially segregated armed forces branches during their time of war. Both experienced and fought against cultural, social, and educational inequity within the country for which they served.

This is primarily the story of James Shipley's military experiences, but in order to have an understanding of the man; one has to understand the factors that helped develop that man. James Shipley's story sets the tone of America, social and cultural relations, and the history within which it was set. Everyone's story contributes to the rich threads of a more fleshed-out history. Telling James Shipley's story provides a glimpse into the life of an individual whose all-but-forgotten service to his country has only recently been recognized and is a prime example of the rich tapestry of life stories yet to be written.

Douglas Shipley
Nephew of James Shipley
Marietta, Georgia
January 2017

Introduction

For several years now, I have had the pleasure of writing a weekly column for the *Jefferson City News Tribune*, which has provided me with the ideal platform to share with the Mid-Missouri community the stories of our local military veterans, many of whom have served during such conflicts as World War II, Korea, Vietnam and the Cold War. While engaged in this endeavor, I have been introduced to many hidden gems throughout Central Missouri—men and women whose legacy of service in a uniform of our nation's armed forces has often gone wholly unnoticed, yet has certainly captured my attention as a story that needs to be preserved.

Sometime in early 2014, I was approached by a coworker regarding a gentleman he knew through his activities at church, a gentleman he identified as Jim Shipley from the rural Mid-Missouri town of Tipton, Missouri. As my coworker went on to inform me, this individual had served with the historic Tuskegee Airmen during World War II, a point of fact that immediately seized my attention since I had never met one of these historic individuals … much less one that was only living miles away from my hometown. Soon, I was provided with Mr. Shipley's telephone number and I made contact with him. During our succinct conversation, I explained to him that I was myself a military veteran and that I pen a weekly newspaper column, then asking whether he would grant me the honor of highlighting his remarkable service as a member of the famed "Red Tails," to which he agreed.

A couple of weeks later, I made the thirty-minute-or-so trip to Tipton and met with Mr. Shipley at the agreed upon location—

Prairie Grove Baptist Church, a historically black congregation that was located directly across the street from the veteran's small and humble home. He explained to me the context of the church's rich history and then took me to one of the back rooms where he had poster boards covered with pictures of the 332nd Fighter Group (Tuskegee Airmen) history that he had constructed for use in presentations to schools and community organizations. After reviewing some of the photographs and newspaper articles he had collected and pasted all over the aged poster boards, we sat down for an interview. I soon realized that not only had Mr. Shipley served in one of the most notable squadrons to emerge from aviation history and helped break down racial barriers that existed in the armed forces during (and prior to) World War II, he also served as an enlisted man—a mechanic—which to me represented a component of the Tuskegee story that is often overlooked since most of the books and stories I have read tend to focus on the officers, or the pilots.

As a young lad growing up in the small, rural community of Russellville, Missouri, I do not remember any racial tensions in my community since I was fortunate be exposed to the wisdom of parents and relatives who did not harbor any discriminatory tendencies or views. Furthermore, though I grew up in a predominately white community, discrimination never seemed a reality because it just did not seem to be a behavior that was either condoned or encouraged.

During my secondary school years and even later in life while researching for homework assignments or articles, I learned about the slaves in Missouri who had been sold into service during the Civil War so that their owners could collect $300 dollars from the government. Many of these recruits went on to serve on behalf of the Union cause in one of several of the Colored Infantry Regiments.[1] Additionally, a number of these black soldiers received

---

[1] The issuance of General Order 135 during the Civil War was the beginning stages of a concentrated effort by the Union Army to recruit men for the United States Colored Troops (USCT). This order, which compensated slave owners up to $300 for each slave they enlisted, not only provided soldiers for the Union cause, but also resulted in the freedom and education of many who had previously lived in bondage. Once many of these former slaves turned combat-hardened soldiers tasted the empowerment of an education while serving in uniform, they often

their freedom after the war and would go on to donate the funds that were later used to finance the establishment of what would become Lincoln University in Jefferson City, embracing the charge to help their fellow black soldiers who possessed the desire to learn to read and write. This, combined with the stories of brave men such as Toney Jenkins—a black veteran from Jefferson City who lost his life while service with the "Harlem Hellfighters"[2] during World War I and later had an American Legion post named in his honor— demonstrated to me that communities in Mid-Missouri honored and respected the dedication and sacrifices of these brave black warriors. With such history, one would like to assume that men like Shipley would have been able to use the honorable service of his black predecessors as a stepping stone into an equality-based U.S. military, but sadly, as history demonstrates, this would not be the case.

Jim's story confirmed that within World War II America there was still a lot of progress to be made in bringing a balance of equality for all of the country's citizens. Despite any lingering hostilities or prejudices that Shipley and his fellow Tuskegee Airmen encountered during their time in uniform, it was a pleasure to listen while he described the professional level of service the Tuskegee Airmen provided the country and the great strides they made in quelling any ill-founded prejudices through the exceptional performance of the many difficult tasks they were given.

When Shipley's story finally appeared in the newspaper, I was not necessarily shocked, but rather pleased with how well it was received by the community. Compliments came flowing in about his

dedicated the rest of their lives to teaching others, leading to the establishment of fine educational institutions such as Lincoln University in Jefferson City—a historically black university.

[2] Born in Jefferson City on October 10, 1894, Toney Jenkins was inducted into the U.S. Army in Fayette, Missouri, on October 29, 1917. Though he trained with the 92nd Division, which earned the title of "Buffalo Soldiers," Jenkins deployed to France with Company G, 369th Infantry Regiment of the 93rd Division, otherwise known as the "Harlem Hellfighters." Jenkins was killed in action during the Meuse-Argonne Offensive on September 28, 1918, becoming the only black veteran from Cole County, Missouri, to lose in life during the war. Missouri Digital Heritage, *Soldiers' Records: War of 1812-WWI*, www.sos.mo.gov/archives.soldiers/.

story, some of which served as inspiration for me to find additional means by which to honor his service. During one of our interviews, I recalled, there had been a moment when Shipley mentioned some hearing loss associated with his exposure to the deafening engines used to power the different types of aircraft he helped maintain during the war, which meant that I had found my instrument through which to accomplish this recognition.

In 2010, I began my involvement with an organization called the Silver Star Families of America (SSFOA)[3] when I was asked to volunteer as their public affairs officer. As part of their mission in supporting the wounded, injured and dying veterans of the nation's armed forces, the SSFOA presents veterans with qualifying military-related injuries a Silver Star Service Banner. Additionally, through working with the Missouri governor's office, I have been able to coordinate the presentation of many of these banners during ceremonies held in the office of the governor at the Missouri Capitol. As such, I requested the banners for Shipley and three other Missouri veterans and was honored to be present when Missouri Governor Jay Nixon made the presentation in the spring of 2014.

Following this event, I returned to my busy schedule of interviewing and writing weekly columns about veterans; however, in early 2015, I made the decision to write a book called *The Lucky Ones* (Burnt District Press, 2016), which chronicled the military service of Henley, Missouri, veteran Norbert Gerling, who had served with Company C, 609th Tank Destroyer Battalion as a gunner aboard an M-18 Hellcat during the Second World War. Sadly, a couple of weeks following the release of this book in January 2016, Gerling passed away.

Prior to Gerling's passing, my intent was to begin work on a book about the Spanish-American War history of Missouri, but as I tried to develop and outline for this project, my thoughts kept returning to the recent loss of Gerling and the alarming rate at which

---

[3] Based upon a tradition originating during World War I, the SSFOA is dedicated to supporting and assisting wounded, ill, injured and dying veterans of all branches of service and from all wars. They recognize the blood sacrifice of those wounded or with injuries and illnesses originating in a warzone by presenting them with the Silver Star Service Banner. Silver Star Families of America website, www.silverstarfamlies.org.

we are losing our World War II heroes. Soon, the focus of my attention shifted to Shipley, and I soon realized that his story was of great historical significance and one that certainly deserved to be preserved through first-hand recollections. In early February 2016, I paid a visit to Shipley's home and told him that I believed his military experience was not something that could simply be relegated to an article and that I would like to write a book about his time with the Tuskegee Airmen, to which he agreed to afford me this glorious opportunity.

I can only hope that through these ensuing pages, I provided an accurate reflection of Shipley's experiences and that his story will in some way resonate with younger generations. Let this, I ask, also serve as a reminder that the men of the 332nd Fighter Group struggled to overcome substantial obstacles to defend the freedoms we continue to enjoy and oftentimes take for granted … even when these black airmen were themselves often denied the same freedoms for which they fought.

In the last several months, Jim Shipley has become many things to me—a hero, an icon, a mentor—but most importantly, he has become a friend. Thank you, Jim, for allowing me to share your story and may God continue to bless you and the men and women who struggled so valiantly to bring equality to the United States military and the nation as a whole.

Jeremy P. Ämick
Russellville, Missouri
January 2017

Chapter 1
Humble Beginnings

"Pit race against race, religion against religion, prejudice against prejudice. Divide and conquer! We must not let that happen here."—Eleanor Roosevelt

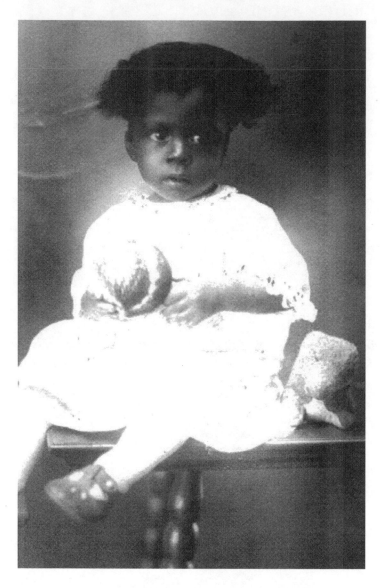

James Shipley is pictured in one of his baby photographs taken sometime in late 1923/early 1924. As was the custom for many young children born in the early 20th century, the young Shipley was wearing a dress in the photograph since they were less complicated to sew and such a design was easier to use when toilet training toddlers.

It is challenging for one to surmise the significant number of twists and turns that can affect the direction of an individual's life journey. A single decision or an unexpected event can result in a person's presence at a certain location or arrival at a specific moment in time that forever changes their life, and thus may inspire others to record for posterity the individual's participation in what becomes a renowned historical event. Understanding the conditions leading to such personal endeavors can bequeath unto us an appreciation for the struggles the person may have overcome to reach such a distinction, while at the same time demonstrating to future generations the magnitude of role this person has played in such an undertaking.

Such is the narrative of James Shipley's unanticipated journey from a rural Missouri community to his valiant service with the renowned Tuskegee Airmen.

Born and raised in Tipton—a predominantly white town in Central Missouri established four years prior to the outbreak of the Civil War— Shipley came of age during a period in American history when black citizens assiduously struggled for equality. However, as Shipley intuitively explained, despite all of the significant changes he has witnessed with regard to race relations in the country he would later enlist to defend, the earliest of his memories are ones full of wonder and excitement: reflections of a childhood when he and his white neighbors joyfully shared in a number of imaginative endeavors as they played together, simply enjoying one another's youthful company while not harnessed with the weight of prejudice that permeated many other communities of the period.

"All of the white kids and all of us black kids from around town ... we all just always seemed to get along great together," Shipley mirthfully recalled. "They would come over to our homes and play marbles with us and we would all just have fun together, sometimes breaking each others' toys, as kids would sometimes do," he added, with hearty laugh.

Born the third of five children at his parents' home in Tipton on June 29, 1923, Shipley described himself as somewhat of a "sickly child" during his early years, often finding it difficult to breathe and burdened with asthma-like symptoms, occasionally lacking the strength and endurance that seemed to power the other children his age.

"When I was younger, I remember that I was able to save enough money to buy this fancy wool-lined coat. It was a big, heavy coat and that thing weighed enough that I couldn't walk to the [nearby] school while I was wearing it or else I would be completely out of breath and have to take it off before I even got there," he earnestly reflected.

A focal point during his years growing up, James Shipley attended Harrison School (pictured in the early 1900s), an all-black school where his father served as a teacher and principal until it closed following desegregation of the public-school system in the late 1950s. Though the building still stands and is owned by the Shipley family, it no longer features the bell tower that was once attached to the roof. **Courtesy of James Shipley**

Galveston Shipley,[4] the young boy's father, helped ensure that his son's earliest memories were ones that revolved around his

---

[4] Galveston Leroy Shipley was born on July 14, 1892 and passed away on March 1, 1978. He is buried in the Prairie Grove Cemetery located one-half mile north of Tipton. Per the Moniteau County Cemetery Book, the Prairie Grove Cemetery was

attendance at a local schoolhouse. Serving as both a teacher and later the principal at the Harrison School, an all-black school in Tipton, Shipley recalls the important role his father served in the earliest of his academic endeavors.

"My father taught at the Harrison School for more than thirty years," said Shipley. "He had told me that there had been an agreement some years back that if the black community would vote in support of a bond that would allow for a new white school to be built in the town, then they would also build a new school for all of the local black students ... and that's how it came to be."

A $12,000 bond issue was placed before Tipton area voters in 1889 to raise the funds to build a school for white children. As part of the bond issue, "$10,000 was used for the construction of a two-story, T-shaped brick grade and high school building for white pupils on the East Morgan Street site and the remaining $2,000 used to erect a building to house the Harrison School ..." wrote Larry Fletcher in *Moniteau County Schools History: 1810-1984*. Harrison School was constructed around 1890 and, during its first year of operation, saw nearly "sixty Negro children enrolled."[5] The school remained in operation until closing in the late 1950s, but the original school building still stands on Howard Street in Tipton and is now owned by the Shipley family.

During his early days as an employee of the school, his father taught all the classes, Shipley explained, which spanned the first through the eighth grades and included a range of subjects such as math, science, reading and writing. In later years, Shipley recalled, a high school course of instruction was also added to the curriculum and another teacher was eventually hired.

"There weren't teachers covering each one of the classes like you have nowadays," Shipley said. "Our school just didn't have the money the other [white] school had and we had to make due with a lot less. I even remember that my dad had to teach the girls how to sew and my mom's parents were the janitors for the school."

once listed as the Tipton Colored Cemetery. Moniteau County, Missouri, *Prairie Grove Cemetery Listings*, www.moniteau.net.
[5] Fletcher, *Moniteau County Schools History*, 55

A young Jim Shipley, far left, is pictured in 1928 with a group of
local children from around the Tipton community, all of whom
would go on to attend Harrison School and receive an education
from Shipley's father, Galveston. At the far right is Shipley's
younger brother, David. **Courtesy of the Dr. David O. Shipley,**
Sr. family.

Shipley's nephew, Douglas, noted that Galveston maintained a keen interest in self-betterment throughout his entire life and "continued to pursue his education while teaching at Harrison School by taking correspondence courses from Lincoln University and later from the University of Missouri." (The University of Missouri admitted its first black students in 1950.) He added, "Apparently, he earned enough credits to receive an undergraduate degree, but never applied for graduation." As Douglas further explained, his grandfather received more of an education than had many of the white residents in the Tipton area and did not want to create unnecessary tensions in an environment already possessing a precarious racial stability.

Although the position Shipley's father held as primary teacher at the school meant he would have more time together with his young son, Shipley noted that it also meant he was less likely have the anonymity that was necessary to engage in any "shenanigans."

"My father was a very stern man and let me tell you—if I cut-up at school, not only did I end up getting a whippin' while I was there, but my dad would give me another whippin' when we got back home," he said, grinning. "Also, my dad never would help me with any of my homework assignments because he always believed that some of the parents of the other kids might claim he was helping me get good grades." Gently, he concluded, "So my mom would be the one to have to help me with my homework in the evenings."

Shipley recalls the long hours his father put in at the school to ensure the black children of Tipton received the best education possible. This investment of time; however, did not elevate the family's income above other black families in the community and necessitated that Shipley's father take on summer work to help make ends meet.

"My father was earning about a quarter of the income the teachers at the white school were making so we were pretty poor while I was growing up," Shipley affirmed. "I can remember getting holes in my shoes just like a lot of the other black kids in town and pulling out the tongue [of the shoe] to fill the hole because my parents couldn't afford to get us new shoes." He added, "My dad didn't get a salary from the school in the summer so he had to take on other jobs like cutting grass and odd jobs around town to help supplement our income; all of this was in between his taking college courses as well. There was a lot of times that we didn't seem him too much during the summer months."

Galveston Shipley is pictured with his wife, Frances, who went by her middle name of Arvenia. Galveston spent a large part of his adult life providing the best education possible for black students in the Tipton community. **Courtesy of James Shipley**

With income often tight, the Shipleys would come together to "work as a family," which included his mother, Frances "Arvenia,"[6] selling "all-black hair products" for a company named Madame C.J .Walkers—a widely known and successful business of the time. In the early 1900s, Madame Walker developed a specialty line of products designed specifically for black hair and skin and employed women to sell her line of products door to door and out of

---

[6] Born in 1898, Frances "Arvenia" Shipley passed away on April 8, 1993 and is buried next to her husband in Tipton's Prairie Grove Cemetery.

their homes. Arvenia also ran a hairdressing businesses out the of family's home, serving local black women, many of whom, Shipley explained, were employed at a local company sewing clothing while others worked as maids and cooks for white families in the area. The black men of the community, he added, found jobs on nearby farms or with the local railroad company, changing sections of track or other laborious tasks. His mother's effort to help provide for her family, Shipley noted, were common among many of the black families in the area but did not raise their standard of living higher than most. However, he concedes that it did instill in him the importance of the role every member of the family played in providing during financially stressful times.

James Shipley, facing the camera and wearing an aviator helmet, is pictured in the early 1930s in front of Harrison School, where his father, Galveston Shipley, standing, served as teacher and principal for several decades. **Courtesy of Douglas Shipley.**

As the years passed and young Shipley grew in strength and in health, and under the tender guidance of his parents, continued to make friends among the white children in the community despite the lingering presence of Jim Crow laws and segregation. Prior to the passage of the Civil Rights Act of 1964, Jim Crow laws "separated Americans by race in 26 states" and resulted in an environment in many locations where "people lived in segregated neighborhoods and attended schools that were all white or all black." Additionally, these laws were often intended to "prevent any possible contact between black and white U.S. citizens out of fear" it might create an environment leading to equal rights for all citizens, also providing many business owners with the legal right to refuse service to a customer based upon their skin color. [7] These laws surfaced in such a manner that prohibited blacks from eating alongside whites in restaurants and other public dining facilities and required them to give white drivers the right-of-way at intersections in addition to leading to the creation of separated bathroom facilities—all of which became an unfortunate reality for young black persons growing up in the early half of the nineteenth century.

As Shipley recalled, one of the most notable examples of division in his community were the railroad tracks, which provided an unspoken separation between two segments of society trying to coexist within the small town of Tipton.

"The black families lived pretty much on the north side of the tracks and the white families on the other side. But that didn't keep all of us kids from playing around together and I don't recall any major racial incidents other than someone occasionally calling a black person a racist name. Even then, there weren't any big fights or hate crimes like I've heard happened in other towns back years ago."

The evidence of segregation was present, however, when visiting one of their local businesses. "Back then, they had 'picture shows'[8] here in town in a place on Main Street that was ran by a company out of Sedalia. If you were black, you were only allowed to set up in the balcony where it was really dark, smoky and noisy." Pausing in reflection, he added, "We knew what we were and weren't allowed to do—you just went along with it because you

---

[7] Tischauser, *Jim Crow Laws*, xi.
[8] Shipley is referring to motion pictures, more commonly known as "movies."

knew that there really wasn't a whole lot that you could do to change the way things were back in those days."

This racial division was also seared into the memory of Shipley's younger brother, the late David O. Shipley. "In our total community, there were always two divisions—white and black, a divided school," he wrote. "Even our town was divided. All of the Negroes lived on one side of town and the whites the other. Whites could move on our side to live although those who did so were regarded by upper-class whites as poor white trash," he sagely described.[9]

Prairie Grove Baptist Church, now located on Howard Street in Tipton, Missouri, was first organized in 1866 by a group of former slaves and is named for the grove of trees where they first met to socialize and worship. **Courtesy of Jeremy P. Ämick**

Though school life and the pursuit of an education was a segregated reality in the lives of Shipley and his siblings, it remains

---

[9] Shipley, *Neither Black Nor White*, 76.

an important focal point in his reflections and became the venue through which he began to identify his interest and abilities in someday becoming a mechanic. Shipley recalls his grandfather, whose full-time employment was a truck driver, hanging large motors from a tree in a yard across the street from the schoolhouse so that they could be rebuilt. During his recess periods, a youthful, exuberant Shipley would bolt across the street and begin the process of tearing down the motors, all the while learning the details associated with repairing and replacing the parts that had been removed.

"I'd run over there, jerk the oil pan off the motor, remove the valve cover and knock the pistons out," he exclaimed. "That's where I first began to learn how to work on engines and I always seemed to enjoy it more than playing baseball or any of the other games all of the kids were playing."

Shipley also joyfully described the many Saturdays as a young boy he spent at a local shoe repair and sales shop operated by George Safire,[10] an immigrant from the Middle East who, according to the *History of Moniteau County Missouri, Volume II*, moved to the community of Tipton in 1932 and "[o]nly his accent hinted at the fact that he was not a native of Tipton."[11] *The Sunday News and Tribune* notes that Safire came to the United States from Beirut, Lebanon on January 5, 1929 and filed for his United States citizenship in early July 1934.[12] Information accessed through the Miller County Museum and Historical Society (which references an article that appeared in the *Eldon Advertiser*) documents that Safire's father, Joseph, also emigrated from Lebanon and operated a

---

[10] George Safire was born in 1904, died in 1990 and is buried in Hillcrest Cemetery in Fulton, Missouri. The *Moniteau County Missouri History* (2000) explains that Safire, his brother and sister shared a house in Lebanon while their father was living in the United States, and that George was employed for the Red Cross Near East Relief for ten years prior to his immigration. It is likely that he was not buried in his hometown of Tipton since he had no descendants when he passed and his brother lived in the community of Fulton. Find A Grave, *George Safire*, www.findagrave.com.

[11] Moniteau County Historical Society, History of Moniteau County, Missouri (Volume II), 589.

[12] July 8, 1934 edition of *The Sunday News and Tribune*.

shoe repair shop in Eldon, Missouri for fifty-three years.[13] Ray Safire, George's brother, was self-employed as a shoe repairman in the community of Fulton, Missouri.

"George [Safire] may have talked a little different than other white folks around Tipton because he was an immigrant, but no one treated him badly or poked fun at him because he was really good at making shoes," Shipley remarked. "He was really a likeable guy and I think that he became so good at his craft that he just earned everyone's respect."

The Moniteau County Historical Society also noted that people would come from all around the Tipton community to buy their boots from Safire because he acquired the reputation of having the ability to correctly guess their boot size without taking any measurements and would then fervently dig through the boxes stacked around his store to locate a pair to fit their feet.

"Me and ol' George became good buddies and he was always very encouraging of me," recalled Shipley. "He would always say, 'That Jimmy, he's alright.' He had a shop off Highway 50 [in Tipton] and he would let me come there on Saturday mornings and shine shoes. I would make a pocket full of money but I had to work hard for it," he bluntly explained. "Those farmers from around the area would come in with cow manure all over their boots but they would walk out of there with those boots just a shinin' like glass!" he proudly declared. "I would spend hours bent over polishing boots and shoes until my back hurt."

He added, "I remember he had three tin cans set up beside his shoe-making equipment. Once he got paid, he put a little of the money in the first can to help pay off the machine, some money in the second can for himself and a little in the third can for his savings." With a broad grin inspired by pleasant reflection, Shipley concluded," That fella was tight [frugal] as they come but I know he had to have a stack of money when he left this world."

In addition to the education he received while attending his local school, Shipley's parents believed it a priority that their children should also understand the importance of a spiritual

---

[13] Miller County Museum, *Eldon Advertiser*, www.millercountymuseum.org/.

education. Situated across the street from the school, the Shipleys were members of the Prairie Grove Baptist Church, which remains an active congregation in the Tipton community and is where Shipley has in later years served as a deacon. Established in 1866, the church, per a history compiled by Shipley's father, was established by former Christian slaves who, after the Civil War, wished to gather for worship at a central assembly site first located in a grove of trees in an area of northeast Tipton. The site of the original church, Shipley's father described in his historical writings, was on a one-acre lot donated by William Tipton Seely, the founder of Tipton himself. [14]

Shipley continued his studies at Harrison School and immersed himself in the learning the intricacies of engine rebuilding while assisting his grandfather in the yard across from the school, but years later, after completing his third year of high school, arrived at a critical juncture in his path toward either continuing his formal education or making his entry into the local workforce.

"Harrison School only went to the eleventh grade and if you wanted to finish high school, you had to ride a bus all the way to Sedalia to complete your final year at an all-black school there," he explained. "Instead, I decided I would go ahead and go to work somewhere because back then you didn't have buses to get you to school; even if you did, it would have taken a long time traveling to get there and back every day."

The C.C. Hubbard High School in Sedalia, of which Shipley referred, was named for Christopher Columbus Hubbard, a native of Glasgow, Missouri. Hubbard once served as principal of Lincoln School in Sedalia, which later grew into what became the Hubbard School. Built in 1928 adjacent to the Lincoln School (which had been built in 1911) the C.C. Hubbard High School has also been recognized as the Lincoln-Hubbard School. It became the "last remaining building in Sedalia, Missouri, to be built and used as a separate school for African-American students."[15] The school had by 1940 "outgrown its local status and had begun to serve out-of-town

---

[14] Shipley, *Centennial History*, www.moniteau.net.
[15] Missouri Department of Natural Resources, *National Register of Historic Places Registration Form: C.C. Hubbard High School*, http://dnr.mo.gov/shpo/nps-nr/97000628.pdf.

students. Students were bused to the school from Marshall, Warrensburg, Versailles, Knobnoster, Tipton, Holden and a host of other towns in the area." [16]

To assist his son in his search for gainful employment since he would not be continuing in his high school studies, Galveston Shipley took advantage of a contact he had made while working for an older woman in the community during one of his summers off from his responsibilities at Harrison School.

"My dad did some house and yard work for a local woman whose son was new to the area and had just opened a [mechanics] garage. He decided to help me out by seeing if he could get me a job."

Galveston Shipley realized that the woman's son, Paul Miller,[17] possessed both the knowledge and resources to train his son in further refining his skills as an automobile mechanic. After Shipley's father approached Miller and inquired about the possibility of his son working at the garage, he agreed to bring the young Shipley on as an employee and soon relied on him to perform various types of tasks that he was unable to accomplish due to physical limitations.

"Miller had a bad back and when my dad went over and talked to him, he convinced him that I would be able to do the mechanic work he might find difficult, like crawling under the cars," Shipley noted. "I wasn't any stranger to working on motors when I started there because of my grandpa," he continued, "but I quickly learned a lot more than I already knew. He was a great mechanic and would tell me what I needed to do to fix something and then he'd inspect my work; he then would also take the time to explain what I did right or," he paused, smiling, "what I *didn't* do right."

---

[16] Nolen, *African Americans in Mid-Missouri*, 94.

[17] Paul H. Miller was born October 15, 1906 and passed away June 1, 1997. He is buried in the cemetery of St. Andrews Catholic Church in Tipton, Mo. Find A Grave, *Paul H. Miller*, www.findagrave.com. In the obituary for Miller's mother, Bertha K. Miller, which was printed in the June 28, 1966 edition of *The Daily Capital News,* it is noted that she served as a teacher in Tipton, which was a connection that both Paul Miller and James Shipley shared—they both had parents that were educators.

The true definition of a full-service shop, Shipley explained, Paul Miller's Garage (which became Miller's Motors in 1940) offered a range of services including body work, painting, carburetor and alternator repair in addition to electrical wiring for trailers and lights.

"I learned how to do it all; it wasn't like it is nowadays where you have a specialist for every little thing that needs to be done. And I remember working on those Model As, Model Ts—old jobs," he said, "even those Whippets[18]! Miller was also a Studebaker dealer, so I learned how to do all the work on those, too. It all worked out wonderfully because I wanted to be a mechanic and there is no way I could have afforded to attend an automotive maintenance and repair school in Kansas City.

After a couple of years assisting Miller at the garage, the budding mechanic decided it was time to jump on the bandwagon that was known as "defense employment" and see if he could locate a position that might offer him the opportunity to make a good salary while at the same time doing his part to support the war effort.

Traveling to Kansas City in 1941, a young Shipley had hopes in acquiring employment in a booming industry—defense manufacturing. Defense plants became a major employment opportunity for many in the Midwest during the Second World War, as one newspaper article mentions there existed three such plants in the Kansas City area, which included the Lake City Army Ammunition Plant, the Sunflower Army Ammunition Plant and the North American Aviation B-25 bomber plant. All combined, these manufactures "employed 78,500 people at their wartime peak."[19] Yet regardless of any available opportunities, Shipley was advised by an employment office that because he was so close to the draft age,[20] he would not be offered a job at that time because an

---

[18] The Whippet was a car once manufactured by the company Willy's-Overland.
[19] Collision, *World War II-era defense plants in Missouri still rev up economy*, December 10, 2010 edition of the *Columbia Missourian*.
[20] Information retrieved from the National Archives notes that President Franklin D. Roosevelt signed the *Selective Training and Service Act* in 1940. This act created "the country's first peacetime draft and officially establishing the Selective Service System" and required all men between the ages of 21 and 45 to register. National Archives, *Selective Service Records*, www.archives.gov. Information from The National World War II Museum shows that "[b]y the end of the war in

employer could not afford to lose a trained employee to military service. Instead, he remained in Kansas City and found a night-shift job performing maintenance on trucks.

"That only lasted about a week," he laughed, "before I figured out I didn't want anything to do with any of that night work. That's when I decided to come back to Tipton and, fortunately, Paul Miller decided to take me back on [as a mechanic]."

For the next year, Shipley continued to gain knowledge and experience working at Paul Miller's Garage, but an event in the fall of 1942 would alter the course of his life and soon place him among a group of men that would earn a revered place in the annals of American military history. While dropping off some mail at the post office in Tipton, Shipley ran into a recruiter for the U.S. Army who was searching for possible enlistees. Then, during their visit, he was informed by the recruiter that the Army was in the process of organizing an "all-black air force" in Tuskegee, Alabama.

"He was positive that I could get a job because they were looking for everything—mechanics, nurses, pilots, radio operators," Shipley excitedly recalled. "I figured that it would be a good opportunity to find out where I stood with things. If I passed their test, then I'd go in the service; if I couldn't pass their test, then I would have a better chance of getting a good-paying defense job [because an employer would not have to worry about later losing their employee to the draft]."

The recruiter instructed the young military prospect on the specific date and time that he was to report to Kansas City to board a bus filled with other black volunteers bound for Ft. Leavenworth, Kansas, where they would then be given their physical examinations.

"There must have been two busloads of us leave out of Kansas City," said Shipley. "[The recruiter] told me to pack enough clothes to last me three days or so," recalled Shipley, recounting a discussion from several decades' past.

1945, 50 million men between eighteen and forty-five had registered for the draft and 10 million had been inducted in the military." National World War II Musuem, *The Draft and World War II,* www.nationalww2museum.org.

Arriving at Ft. Leavenworth in early November 1942, the young recruit spent the next few days undergoing physical evaluations, testing and was interviewed about the skills he had developed as a mechanic in his hometown. His boss, Paul Miller, was supportive of Shipley's desire to serve and had written his employee a letter of recommendation outlining the abilities Shipley had developed in his previous two years of employment at his garage.

"It was kind of an interesting experience because while I was there, I saw young guys break down and cry because they couldn't pass the physical … they really wanted to join," said Shipley, describing the entrance processing for the Tuskegee recruits. "Some of them found out they had heart trouble and things like that," he added.

Prior to Shipley making the decision to sign his enlistment papers, there had been several events that fell into place and great strides that were made by African Americans and others struggling for equality within both military and civilian sectors; individuals who had simply sought to create an environment that would provide the opportunity for men like Shipley to prove their mettle in service to their country as part of the Tuskegee Airmen.

Although there exist scores of intricate and interesting moving parts that intertwine and serve as an advent to the Tuskegee story, one of the most fascinating is that of the contributions made by Eugene Jacques Bullard.

Born in Columbus, Georgia in1894, Bullard would become the first black American aviator; however, it would be an accomplishment that would not take place in his native land of America, but rather in his newly adopted home of France. Immigrating to Europe at the tender age of twelve after hearing stories that he might find equality amongst the French people, Bullard went on to join the French Foreign Legion in 1914. During the First World War, he experienced heavy combat and was wounded on March 5, 1916. Found to be unfit for infantry duty, Bullard was accepted into the French Flying Corps and earned his aviation wings on May 5, 1917. He went on to fly many missions on behalf of the French government but by the time the United States entered the war in 1917, Bullard was denied transfer to the air force of the United States although "he had fought for over three years in the war and been wounded four times, twice in the battle of Verdun."[21] In addition to having spent eight months in the hospital recovering from wounds, the aviator earned many medals for valor for his service to the French; yet because of his skin color and despite his service as a fighter pilot in a French squadron, he was not given the opportunity to serve as a pilot for the U.S. Army Air Service.

During the First World War, Eugene Jacques Bullard learned to fly and France and went on to become a fighter pilot with a French squadron, receiving both combat wounds and medals for valor during his service. U.S. Air Force photograph

---

[21] Chivalette, *Corporal Eugene Jaques Bullard*, www.airpower.maxwell.af.mil.

There were many obstacles in the ensuing years for aspiring black aviators to surmount, but the efforts of inspired individuals such as John C. Robinson went to great lengths in confirming the abilities as African-Americans to serve as aviators. Though Robinson's name has become shrouded in relative obscurity, he gained a significant level of fame in the mid-1930s by serving as the commander of the Imperial Ethiopian Air Force during the Italo-Ethiopian War.

A graduate of the Tuskegee Normal and Industrial Institute (which later became Tuskegee Institute), Robinson would excel more in studies related to mechanical science than any other subject and made the "noteworthy achievement [that] was a groundbreaking class project in which he led a group of his fellow students in building a working automobile."[22]

Years later, he became the first black student admitted to the renowned Curtiss-Wright School of Aviation in Chicago where he studied aviation mechanics and later became a teacher. Prior to his service in Ethiopia, Robinson became a notable pilot and tirelessly advocated for Tuskegee to become the site to train black aviators, which would later become a reality. Some historians note that the beginnings of Tuskegee's entry into aviation training can be traced to Robinson and the "Tuskegee alumnus flying an airplane to his class reunion as early as 1934 [which] must have profoundly impacted perceptions of the opportunities offered by the airplane."[23]

---

[22] Tucker, *Father of the Tuskegee Airmen: John C. Robinson*, 22.
[23] Brady, *The American Aviation Experience*, 347.

John C. Robinson was once referred to as the "black Lindbergh," and helped pave the way for black aviators through his association with the Curtiss-Wright Aeronautical School and later distinguished himself with the Imperial Ethiopian Air Force in the Italo-Ethiopian War. Public Domain

As noted in the *Tuskegee Airmen Chronology* by Dr. Daniel Haulman, as early as 1939, the structure of an all-black Air Force began to fall into place with the Congressional passage of the Civilian Pilot Training Act, followed by other critical events such as the Civil Aeronautics Administration's approval of Tuskegee Institute as a civilian pilot training institution weeks later. The passage of the *Selective Service Act* by Congress on September 16, 1940, Dr. Haulman explains, would require the "armed services to enlist 'Negroes'" and the War Department would the same day announce "that the Civil Aeronautics Authority, in cooperation with the U.S. Army, would start the development of 'colored personnel' for the aviation service."[24]

This drive toward equality in the armed forces was propelled further forward in October 1940 when the administration of President Franklin Roosevelt made the announcement that blacks would be trained as military pilots in the Army Air Corps. Additionally efforts spearheaded by National Association for the Advancement of Colored People (NAACP), an organization which grew exponentially in membership during the war, also helped ensure that black aviators would someday play an integral in helping the United States succeed in the war. The culmination of these efforts soon began to take form in January 1941 when the War Department's decided they would create an all-black pursuit squadron and begin training pilots at Tuskegee, Alabama, followed by the formation of the 99th Pursuit Squadron at Chanute Field, Illinois, two months later.

The year prior to Shipley's enlistment was a frenetic point in the history of the black aviation squadrons as the first class of aviation cadets entered their pre-flight training at Tuskegee in July 1941, which included such renowned individuals as Benjamin Oliver Davis, Jr. Born in Washington, D.C., in 1912, Davis would go on to become an icon in the annals of military history, particularly to African Americans. He attended both Western Reserve University and University of Chicago, but later graduated from the U.S. Military Academy at West Point, New York in 1932. In the years prior to World War II, he served as a commander of an infantry

---

[24] Haulman, *Tuskegee Airman Chronology*, 1.

company at Ft. Bragg, North Carolina and later became professor of military science at Tuskegee Institute.

Benjamin O. Davis, Jr. served as professor of military science at Tuskegee Institute and, in May 1942, earned his pilot wings. During World War II, he served as commander of the 99th Fighter Squadron and would later earn the distinction as the first African-American general officer in the United States Air Force. **U.S. Air Force photograph**

While at Tuskegee, he earned his pilot wings in March 1942, was commander of the 99th Fighter Squadron and served with his unit in North Africa, Sicily and Italy. In the years after World War II, Davis served in several capacities and locations with the U.S. Air Force, retiring from active military service at the rank of lieutenant general in 1970. On December 9, 1998, Davis was advanced to the rank of four-star general by President Clinton. Sadly, the former Tuskegee Airman passed away on July 4, 2002.[25]

Months after Davis entered his pre-flight training at Tuskegee; the Japanese attacked Pearl Harbor in Hawaii, an event that immediately increased the need for combat pilots. The war in Europe raged for more than two years before the United States was drawn into the fray but on the morning of December 7, 1941, hundreds of Japanese planes attacked the American naval base at Pearl Harbor near Honolulu, Hawaii—a singular event that deprived the base of "air protection and inflicted heavier damage on the United States Navy than had been suffered in all of World War I." The following afternoon, the United States Senate and House of Representatives met at a joint session in the nation's Capital during which President Franklin Roosevelt asked that "Congress declare that since the unprovoked and dastardly attack by Japan on Sunday, December 7, a state of war has existed between the United States and the Japanese Empire." That same afternoon, the Senate and House both adopted resolutions declaring a state of war with Japan, with President Roosevelt signing the declaration at 4:10 p.m.[26]

Even with the country issuing a call for all available hands to assist with the bourgeoning war effort, aspiring black recruits still faced an uphill battle in acquiring equality in the armed forces. Training manuals for white officers such as *Leadership and the Negro Soldier* had only helped to perpetuate many faulty myths, often portraying black soldiers as "shiftless and lazy," or even going so far as describing them as" cowardly—he would run from combat if put in the line of fire."[27]

---

[25] U.S. Air Force Biography, *General Benjamin O, Davis Jr.*, www.af.mil.
[26] Miller, *History of World War II*, 310.
[27] Morehouse, *Fighting in the Jim Crow Army*, 133.

Posters, such as the one pictured above from 1943, were created by the military during World War II to appeal not only to the country at large, but oftentimes specifically to the African American community. **National Museum of the U.S. Air Force**

The result of a 1925 initiative by the Army War College to evaluate the fitness of black soldiers for continued service in the military (primarily in combat), the study all but dismissed the stellar performance of African-Americans in all wars since before the country's founding and became a tool used by certain military leaders to argue against any future attempts to desegregate the military. African-Americans in the armed forces remained segregated from their white counterparts but would soon be placed in situations that provided them opportunity to once again prove themselves in a combat environment.

While the training at Tuskegee continued in earnest to train black aviation personnel, on November 7, 1942, with his list of entrance processing requirements completed, Shipley signed his enlistment papers and became a member of the United States Army Air Forces only three days prior to the graduation of the eighth class of African Americans from flight training at Tuskegee Institute. He had taken the first step in becoming one of more than "a half a million black soldiers [to serve] during the war, with about 80,000 going overseas."[28]

A young man from small the town of Tipton thus embarked on a fascinating journey that would soon cast him into the center of a great adventure as a member of one of the most respected military organizations to emerge from World War II. Little did Shipley realize at the time, he and his counterparts would help pave the way for all African Americans with a desire to serve in the armed forces of the United States. Soon, he and his fellow recruits would "prove beyond any conceivable question that black Americans could fly and maintain some of the world's most sophisticated killing machines, lead and staff complicated bureaucratic systems, and excel under tremendous pressure." [29]

[28] Parkerson, *Transitions in American Education*, 49.
[29] Moye, *Freedom Flyers*, 40.

Chapter 2
From Tipton to Tuskegee

"Associate yourself with people of good quality, for it is better to be alone than in bad company". –Booker T. Washington

Staff Sergeant Shipley is pictured in uniform shortly after returning home from his service in Italy during the Second World War.

Upon his enlistment, Shipley and a group of his fellow black recruits boarded a train at Ft. Leavenworth, Kansas and embarked on their journey to Tuskegee, Alabama, where only months earlier, the first class of black pilots had graduated on March 7, 1942 from their basic and advanced flight training course at the flying school at Tuskegee Army Airfield (TAAF). Though TAAF was operated by the military, the nearby Tuskegee Institute contracted with the military to provide boot camp and primary flight training for the black aviation personnel in the U.S. Army Air Forces[30] and established their own airfield known as Moton Field.

The Tuskegee Institute was established in the 1880s to educate African American students with Booker T. Washington being hired by the founders to serve as the first head of the institute. During the Second World War, the institute was chosen "to train pilots for the war effort because Tuskegee had the facilities, engineering and technical instructors and a climate well suited for year-round flying."[31]

Named for Robert Russa Moton, the second president of Tuskegee Institute, the nearby Moton Field was "built between 1940-1942 with funding from the Julius Rosenwald Fund to provide primary flight training under a contract with the U.S. military." Once the black cadets completed their primary flight training at Moton, they were transferred to Tuskegee Army Air Field for more advance levels of military aviation training. Though Moton Field has long since closed, much of the airfield is now used by the city of Tuskegee for their municipal airport.[32]

---

[30] The successor to the U.S. Army Air Corps, the U.S. Army Air Forces was formed in 1941in response to the growing structure and mission that Army aviators were playing and the need for a more independent command structure." As noted on the U.S. Army website, by the time World War II unfolded, many nations had already established air forces independent of their armies; however, aviators would remain part of the U.S. Army until the establishment of the United States Air Force in 1947. U.S. Army, *Army Aviation*, www.army.mil.

[31] National Park Service, *Tuskegee Airmen National Historic Site*, www.nps.gov.

[32] National Park Service, *Legends of Tuskegee: Moton Field*, www.nps.gov.

"The day that we got to Tuskegee," recalled Shipley, "there were [black] soldiers everywhere … as far as you could see. Coming from such a small town, I had never seen so many black people in one place at one time. It was really hard to believe just how big a base it really was and how far it stretched."

While Shipley and his fellow recruits were on the ground completing basic training and "mopping up mud puddles," they frequently saw planes such as the Boeing PT-17 Stearman—a military training aircraft—in the skies above being used in the training of black aviation cadets. U.S. Air Force photograph

While completing his basic training at Tuskegee Army Air Field, Shipley was assigned to a "tent city" upon his arrival, but toward the latter part of his training stayed in barracks similar to the ones pictured. Air Force Historical Research Agency, Maxwell Air Force Base photo collection

Shipley's perception of the frenetic activity on the Alabama base was precise, as the book *Freedom Flyers: The Tuskegee Airmen of World War II* notes that "[by] the end of 1942 TAAF was home to nearly 3,500 officers, enlisted men, pilot cadets, and civilian employees—a more than twenty-fold increase in one year's time—and it was still growing."[33]

Soon after his arrival, the nineteen-year-old recruit underwent the conventional in-processing for a trainee by receiving his assignment to a tent, signing for his standard issue of military clothing, "falling out for chow" and preparing to embark upon the beginning of his basic training at the segregated post. The men in his training battalion, Shipley noted, were all enlisted soldiers destined to become aviation maintenance personnel of some sort, many of whom would remain together throughout all of their military training and even during their eventual deployment overseas.

---

[33] Moye, *Freedom Flyers*, 94.

The morning following his arrival at Tuskegee, Shipley and the scores of other recruits were awakened at reveille (a bugle call played on military bases—generally at sunrise—to signal troops to assemble for roll call) and lined up in a formation outside of their barracks for a head count. It was at this point they received a rather gruff introduction to the man who would be solely responsible for their military instruction throughout the next several weeks.

"That's when they assigned us to this old lieutenant ... he looked like he was fifty or sixty years old, which seemed ancient to us because we were all nineteen or so," he grinned. "He was an old infantry guy and we all thought that we had it made and that he wouldn't be able to put us through much physical activity, but that old man took us on a hike for several miles on the very first day in training. He would walk us for awhile and then run us for a little while ... and I tell you what" he exclaimed, "that old man wore us out and it didn't take us very long to change our minds about him— he was in great shape!"

His time in training at Tuskegee not only found him embroiled him in all aspects of the military lifestyle, which included time spent firing rifles on one of the post ranges and learning to maneuver obstacle courses, but it also served as his introduction to a fellow recruit that would become a close friend and with whom he would spend nearly his entire period of military service.

"James D. Ross[34] was from somewhere around Tuskegee and a few years older than me," shared Shipley. "He had worked at an Army hospital before the war, I believe, and volunteered like me to serve; he wasn't drafted. Any time we went out on maneuvers, we would share our tents. (At that time, Shipley explained, soldiers were issued a canvas shelter that was known in military lexicon as a "pup tent." Two soldiers would carry enough equipment to form a single tent, with two canvas pieces that would snap together and then supported with the necessary ropes and poles).

---

[34] According to information retrieved from the National Archives, James D. Ross was married when he enlisted in the Army on November 3, 1942. His occupation was at the time listed as "Skilled Mechanics and Repairmen, Motor Vehicles," which would have made him an ideal recruit for an airplane mechanic with the 332nd Fighter Group.

He added, "We were always together during our training and even when we went overseas. He was a pretty tall guy—like six-foot-one or two," he said. "I was quite a bit shorter—five-foot-four back then—and the other soldiers thought our height difference was funny and started calling us *Mutt and Jeff*." [35]

While the black aviation cadets were completing their primary and basic flight training aboard aircraft such as the PT-13, PT-17 and PT-19 at nearby   Moton Field, Shipley was relegated to watching them from on the ground as their "old lieutenant" daily continued to put the group of raw recruits through the paces. The seasoned and aged officer though he might have been, Shipley explained, they were being prepared for potential service in an overseas combat environment; however, he jovially added, there were also occasions during which the point of the exercise being performed was not quite evident.

"We did calisthenics every day," said Shipley, "and went to the rifle ranges and did marksmanship training as well. But one incident that really seems to stand out in my mind is the day we were out on drill, walking down a road in formation. In front of us," he continued," there was this big mud puddle and, like most people would, we all decided that we would do the smart thing and just march right on around it."

Although the training company might have believed they were acting in a competent manner by avoiding the filthy pool of water, their lieutenant was in no way impressed, as Shipley affirmed.

"That ol' lieutenant yelled for us to back up and then told us we were going to march back and forth through that puddle until we dried it up—and we did!" he laughed.

Sometime during his training cycle, the young recruit was assigned to the 301st Fighter Squadron under the 332nd Fighter

---

[35] *Mutt and Jeff* was a comic strip created by cartoonist Bud Fischer. The cartoon enjoyed an immense level of success and popularity during its seventy-five year run and featured the character of Mutt, who was "[t]all and thin, with a bristly mustache and face oddly liking a chin"—the character whose height was used to jokingly identify him as Shipley's friend, James D. Ross. In the comic, Mutt's friend Jeff was smaller in stature and is who Shipley was identified as by his friends and fellow soldiers. Booker, *Comics Through Time*, 265.

Group, with whom he would remain a member during the duration of his time in the U.S. Army Air Forces. The group fell under the command of the Twelfth Air Force, which at the time consisted of the 100th, 301st, 302nd Fighter Squadrons. These three squadrons would later join with the 99th Fighter Squadron (who would fly missions over North Africa, Sicily and Italy) to make the 332nd the largest fighter group when they transferred to their new command under the Fifteenth Air Force in May 1944.

Pictured is the emblem of the 301st Fighter Squadron, with whom Shipley served during the war. The squadron was constituted on July 4, 1942 and activated on October 13, 1942. **Public Domain**

As tends to be the case within many fraternal environments, there were many stories circulating among the young trainees— some grounded in fact while others appeared to be based more upon legend. However, one story that seemed to resonate with a young Shipley was an actual encounter that took place at Tuskegee in March 1941, which, he explained, eventually resulted in the overseas deployment of black pilots who many believed, had fallen into a never-ending cycle of combat training and preparation.

"Eleanor Roosevelt visited Tuskegee," Shipley said, "and while she was there, she asked for one of the pilots to take her up in a plane. Of course, there were a couple of [white] training pilots there who volunteered to take her on a flight, but she pointed to one of the black pilots and said that she wanted him to be the pilot to take her up."

In the book *The Divided Skies: Establishing Segregated Flight Training at Tuskegee, Alabama,* the authors detail this encounter, verifying one of the most profound moments in the annals of black aviation history.

Prior to her visit to the airfield at Tuskegee Institute, the book described, the first lady had been advised that blacks couldn't fly, but she in turn became "determined to demonstrate her confidence in the flying ability of blacks" and requested that C. Alfred Anderson[36]—the chief instructor pilot at Tuskegee—take her for a flight despite the ardent concerns expressed by her aides.

---

[36] Born February 9, 1907 in Pennsylvania, C. Alfred Anderson acquired a fascination with aviation while growing up and would later purchased his own plane, teaching himself to take off and land the aircraft. In 1929, he earned his pilot's license and three years later became the first black pilot to earn his air transport license through the assistance of a German aviator. Throughout the next several years, Anderson participated in several goodwill tours to promote aviation among the black community and served as a flight instructor at Howard University. In 1940, he became the Chief Civilian Flight Instructor at the Tuskegee Institute and then the Chief Instructor for aviation cadets of the 99th Pursuit Squadron. In the years following the war, Anderson provided flight training to both black and white students and even sold aircraft in the Southeast and Southwestern U.S. The black aviation pioneer passed away on April 13, 1996 in Tuskegee, Alabama. National Aviation Hall of Fame, *Charles Alfred "Chief" Anderson,* www.nationalaviation.org.

Anderson spent an hour piloting Mrs. Roosevelt over the Alabama skies, which, history notes, so impressed upon the first lady the abilities of black pilots, it would result in a considerable amount of positive press and financial support for the aviation training site. [37]

Chief Civilian Flight Instructor Charles Alfred Anderson is pictured in the cockpit of a plane with First Lady Eleanor Roosevelt, whom he took on an hour-long flight during her 1941 visit to the Tuskegee Institute. Air Force Historical Research Agency

"After Mrs. Roosevelt visited Tuskegee, remember being told that she went back and told someone at the White House that the black pilots and crews were ready to go," Shipley boldly stated.

It is not entirely certain whether Mrs. Roosevelt's tour at Tuskegee Institute directly resulted in the eventual deployment of the 99th Fighter Squadron, but it was not until early April 1943 that the squadron began their journey overseas where they would spend the first few months in North Africa training for the combat missions they hoped they would soon be given the opportunity to support.

[37] Jakeman, *The Divided Skies*, 246-248.

More than a year following Mrs. Roosevelt's historic visit, Shipley and many of his fellow trainees completed their basic training in the waning days of 1942 and began to scatter to different locations throughout the United States where they would embark upon their advanced training in specific specialties—locations which included sites such as Chanute Field, Illinois (the base where the 99th Fighter Squadron was first activated); Keesler Field, Mississippi; Midland Army Air Field in Texas; Fort Monmouth, New Jersey; and the Curtis-Wright Factory Training School in Buffalo, New York. As a member of the 301st Fighter Squadron, Shipley accompanied many of his fellow trainees (who had just completed their initial training) to Lincoln, Nebraska, one of several military posts where the black trainees were segregated from their white counterparts even while they underwent similar training to become aircraft mechanics.

During the war, the call for mechanics and maintenance personnel became critical as an estimated four technical specialists were required for each man who flew a plane. Additionally, "[t]he ratio of total ground personnel to total flying personnel was nearly seven to one, and for every man actually committed to air combat there were sixteen individuals who served within the AAF [Army Air Forces] on some noncombat assignment." [38] The role played by Tuskegee and the various aviation schools situated throughout the United States were essential in ensuring trained and qualified personnel were available to fly combat missions in both Europe and the Pacific throughout the war.

"When they shipped us to Lincoln, Nebraska [in late December 1942], we were all still wearing our khaki uniforms because it had still been kind of warm when we left Alabama," Shipley explained. Emitting a grin that belied the difficulties of his past experiences, the veteran meekly added, "As soon as we got to Lincoln, they had a blizzard. The first few days we were there we almost froze to death, until they finally got around to issuing us some winter uniforms and clothes."

---

[38] Craven & Cate, *The Army Air Forces in World War II*, 629.

During their training at Lincoln Army Air Field in Nebraska, Shipley and his fellow mechanics learned to perform certain types of repairs and maintenance while operating in a field environment outside of a shop. Pictured are mechanics of the 332nd Fighter Group changing a damaged propeller on a P-51 Mustang while stationed in Ramitelli, Italy in 1944, which was one of many repairs Shipley was trained to perform. Courtesy of Jim Shipley

Shipley, center, pauses for a photograph with two of his fellow trainees during the latter part of his basic training at Tuskegee, Alabama. Courtesy of James Shipley

Assigned to the aircraft mechanics school with the 789th Technical School Squadron, Shipley spent several weeks at Lincoln Army Air Field—a 2,750-acre property leased to the United States Army by the city of Lincoln. The new air field was constructed in 1942 on the former site of the Lincoln Municipal Airport, the State Historical Society of Nebraska notes, and was home to the school that "provided technical training for aircraft mechanics, basic training for army aviation cadets, and served as an overseas deployment staging area for bombardment groups and fighter squadrons." Additionally, the society explained, the air field was one of eleven US. Army Air Forces training centers built in the state during the war.[39]

"They had different kinds of aviation classes all over the base but they were all segregated," shared Shipley. "The Army had opened up a school there for the P-40s and that's where I began to learn to work on those [Allison V-1710] engines," he maintained. More than 70,000 Allison V-1710 engines were manufactured "from the time of the first in 1931 to the last in 1948."[40] Additionally, the seemingly ubiquitous engine saw service in several models of aircraft other than the P-40 Warhawk, including the P-38 Lightning, P-38 Airacobra, P-51A Mustang, P-63 Kingcobra, P-82 Twin Mustang and the and the Consolidated XA-11A.

"There was about forty of us in a class and you learned to tear the engines down, attach the wings on the planes and all of that sort of thing ... and they also taught you how to check it all over, too. Those engines were greasy from all of the oil leaks," he declared, "because everything that we were given to work on was hand-me-downs because all of the good stuff was going in the planes being used in the war." With a beaming grin, he boisterously declared, "One thing they taught us right away is that you don't call it a motor—it's an engine!"

The aviation support personnel undergoing training did not all possess the same mechanical background as Shipley. Some, he explained, would benefit from what he described as "endless patience" of the personnel teaching their courses of instruction.

"There were some of the guys in our training classes who didn't even know what a Phillips screwdriver or needle-nose pliers were," Shipley explained. "But the guys who were teaching us took the time to show us all the tools and explained in detail what the function of each tool was and then demonstrated how it was supposed to be used." He added, "I have to say, I always believed that the training we received was always topnotch and we all took

---

the time to help each other out to make sure we made it through the training alright. As I remember," he concluded, "nobody washed out of any of the training courses because we always worked as a team."

Recalling when he in-processed into the military at Fort Leavenworth, Shipley noted that he and his fellow recruits were asked a series of questions as to the type of work they wanted to perform. Based upon this experience, Shipley surmised that many of those placed in an aviation maintenance field may have expressed a desire to serve as an aircraft mechanic, which was then granted by the Army Air Forces despite their not having any previous experience to support such a placement.

Undergoing several months of intense instruction on the maintenance of the aircraft, Shipley also recalled the many hours he and his fellow mechanic trainees spent in a field environment away from the comfort of an enclosed shop, learning to perform integral repairs such as the replacement of propellers.

There were certain inspections that we had to perform on the airplanes at routine and specific intervals –50 hours, 100 hours, and so on and so forth," he remarked. "It was all set forth in the manuals we used but you did this type of work so often that you were eventually able to memorize it all."

" Not all of the young mechanics' time was spent in training, Shipley explained, since he and other trainees "could go to the mess hall at about anytime [they] were able to break away from what [they] were doing." He jokingly added, "And it always seemed like we ate well … I don't really recall seeing too many skinny soldiers running around there."

On Saturdays, groups of the young mechanic and maintenance students would make their way into the city of Lincoln to dine in different restaurants and occasionally "look at girls," he smiled; but on Sundays, they could be found worshipping at different churches in the area.

"Segregation was something that we were aware of wherever we were at," he said. "When we went into town, we always stayed in the black section of town. Everyone knew how things were back then and we didn't go anywhere looking to start any kind of trouble."

This U.S. Air Force photograph shows mechanics from the 332nd Fighter Group performing engine maintenance on a P-40 Warhawk while stationed at Selfridge Field in a photograph likely taken in 1943. U.S. Air Force photograph

In addition to the many classes in maintenance and repair of aircraft that were provided to Shipley and the other men with whom he trained, several of the young recruits also received an important lesson as to why it was important for a member of the military to think twice before volunteering one's services in the military.

"Yes, I made the mistake of volunteering for KP (kitchen police) just one time," he chuckled. "That ol' mess sergeant that was running the kitchen, he put us to work polishing the floors and we thought we had done a good job and were finished. Well," he continued, "we thought we were going to be able to catch a show that evening but when that sergeant came back in, he went over and turned on a faucet and flooded the entire floor of the room we had just worked so hard to polish. Then he told us to 'Mop her up and you can go.' We eventually got it done but we missed the show. But," he exclaimed, "that's when I made up my mind that I would never volunteer for anything in the service ever again!"

While stationed in Nebraska, Shipley encountered many occasions to become intimately familiar with the Curtiss P-40 Warhawk, which was the fighter plane available in greatest numbers when the United States made its entry into World War II. Before production of the plane was terminated in 1944, a total of 11,998 P-40s were built, ensuring the aircraft would become a primary component of the frenetic training regimen for scores of aviation mechanics and pilots within the U.S. Army Air Forces. [41]

Produced in many variants throughout the duration of the war, the P-40 became an aircraft that the Curtiss-Wright Corporation manufactured in a steady stream for not only the U.S. Army and Navy, but was exported to many Allied nations as well. The aircraft would initially see combat in North Africa but "never reached the performance levels of the later-model Bf-109[42] or Spitfire,[43]" ; however, "the sturdy airplane nevertheless made a place in history for itself as the Army's frontline fighter when the US entered World War II."[44] The aircraft would also serve as a critical component in defining and demonstrating the Tuskegee pilots' ability to respond to the threats of enemy aircraft all while being supported by the well-trained mechanics and ground crewmen such as Shipley, who often worked night and day just to keep them flying.

***

Several months of immersion in all necessary mechanical aspects of the P-40s were soon followed by weeks of applied training at Selfridge Field, Michigan. Named for an Army aviator, Lt. Thomas E. Selfridge[45]—who earned the unfortunate distinction

---

[41] HistoryNet, *Curtiss P-40 Warhawk*, www.historynet.com.

[42] A German fighter plane also known as the Messerschmitt Bf-109 or Me 109.

[43] A single-seat fighter aircraft that was used by the Royal Air Force and other Allied nations during World War II.

[44] Molesworth, *Curtiss P-40*, 5.

[45] The plane on which Selfridge was a passenger was piloted by Orville Wright and crashed on September 17, 1908 during Army performance tests being conducted a Ft. Myer, Virginia. The crash, which caused Selfridge's death, also resulted in several weeks of hospitalization for Wright. Selfridge was laid to rest

of becoming the first casualty of military flight in 1908—the air field was established in May 1917. It was reported that "[d]uring the summer of 1917, 72 men won aviator ratings and logged over 3,700 flying hours" and, in 1922, became a "permanent U.S. military installation under the command of Major Carl "Tooey" [46]Spaatz,[47] who one day would become the first Chief of Staff of the United States Air Force."

Selfridge Field, which later became known as Selfridge Air Force Base and is now home to Selfridge Air National Guard Base, grew to almost five times its original size "[b]etween the attack on Pearl Harbor and the end of 1942," expanding from its original 641 acres to 3,000 acres.[48]

During the time Shipley spent at the air field, it gained the regrettable distinction of being "the scene of racial unrest ..." Major General Frank Hunter, who served as the commander of the First Air Force, issued an order in late 1943 that prohibited black officers from using the officers' club on Selfridge—an order which was deemed by many of the black troops to be in direct violation of Army Regulation 201-10, "which specifically stated that all officers on a post could be members of officers clubs, messes, and similar social organizations."[49] In contestation of their exclusion from the officers' club, nearly one hundred black officers participated in a sit-

---

in Arlington National Cemetery. Arlington, *Thomas Etholen Selfridge*, www.arlingtoncemetery.net.

[46] Mount Clemens Public Library, *The Founding of Selfridge Field*, www.mtclib.org.

[47] Carl A. Spaatz enjoyed a lengthy and distinguished career, which began in the U.S. Army and ended with the newly formed U.S. Air Force. Born in Boyertown, Pennsylvania in 1891, he attended the U.S. Military Academy and began his career as a second lieutenant of infantry. He would go on to serve during World War I and, during the Second World War, served in such capacities as commanding general of the 12th Air Force, commander of the Northwest African Air Force, deputy commander of the Mediterranean Allied Air Forces and commander of the U.S. Strategic Air Forces in Europe. He retired at the rank of general on June 30, 1948 and was the recipient of the Distinguished Flying Cross, Legion of Merit and Bronze Star Medal. General Spaatz passed away on July 14, 1974 at 83 years of age and is interred at the U.S. Air Force Academy near Colorado Springs, Colorado. United States Air Force, *Biography of General Carl A. Spaatz*, www.af.mil.

[48] A TACOM History, *Building a Base: Selfridge and the Army*, 31-32.

[49] Harris, *The Tuskegee Airmen*, 97-98.

in and were later "arrested and threatened with court-martial, but they held their ground and the charges were dropped."[50]

Though Shipley was an enlisted man and the plight experienced by the black officers might not have appeared to be of direct consequence to him, it soon became the clarion call that united many of the black officers to contest the inequalities permeating the post and would later result in non-violent protests that provided the Tuskegee Airmen with a level of equal opportunity and fairness that had been missing in the military.

"[Selfridge] is where we were all assigned to support a specific airplane and a pilot, and then they taught us all of our duties and responsibilities while we worked on the flight line," Shipley said. "The pilots would spend their time practicing their flying under different conditions and our job was to keep the plane in the air ... to keep everything running smoothly as best we were able," he added. "If your plane came in with a miss in the engine, you'd stick your hands right down there into that hot engine and take the plugs out to try and get it back in the air as quickly as you could. Also," he continued, "when the pilot came down for the day, you had to not only check everything out on the plane, but it also had to be gassed up and ready to go for the next day of training."

As Shipley explained, they were still working with P-40s while at Selfridge and the mechanics would occasionally encounter mechanical problems such as those related to wheel struts that would not retract or vibrations that might indicate a propeller was out of balance and needed to be replaced—a procedure, he again noted, they were required to perform in a "field environment" since they might not have the benefit of working from a shop when deployed overseas.

"The pilots were practicing every day—dog fighting, strafing and learning how to perform bombing runs," he said. "They kept us all very busy and there were some really long days just trying to make sure that everything remained in operational condition." He added, "In the mornings, you'd go over the plane completely, which was a process that included starting start engine and checking for oil

---

[50] Bracey, *Daniel "Chappie" James*, 39.

leaks, listening to the sound of the engine and just making sure everything was running all right. You'd even walk around the plane and look for such obvious problems as chunks missing from the tires."

Similar to their time spent at Lincoln, the men of the 332nd occasionally received some time off from their intense training regimen and were authorized to visit the local USO, which regularly scheduled different types of entertainment. The United Service Organizations (USO) "was brought into existence through Presidential order February 4, 1941" and "originally intended to offer assistance only in communities that could not support the great influx of service personnel ..." Throughout World War II, the USO helped provide and oversee recreational services and aid to the military, establishing clubs that provided "lively entertainment like dances, sporting tournaments, and outings." In more recent decades, the USO has expanded to offer mobile services and lounges and assistance for military members who are traveling.[51]

"It was a USO that was specifically for the black soldiers," he remarked, "and we would go there to play games, meet up with other black soldiers and sometimes they would host dinners for us. Also," he further noted, "they would often host dances where we could meet some of the local girls," he meekly grinned.

The opportunities for relaxation only appeared as a brief respite during the frenzied cycle of training the squadron underwent. The days passed quickly as both the pilots and the ground crew continued to refine their combat skills, preparing for the day that they would have to prove their mettle in combat against a dedicated and determined enemy. In early January 1944, they received word that this moment was approaching as the 332nd discovered they would soon make their entry into the deadly conflict that was being fought overseas.

---

[51] WW2 USO, *United Service Organizations*, www.ww2uso.org.

Chapter 3

The Adventure Begins ...

"My own opinion was that blacks could best overcome racist attitudes through achievements, even though those achievements had to take place within the hateful environment of segregation." – General Benjamin O. Davis

Their preparatory combat and mechanical training completed, Shipley and the soldiers of the 332nd boarded troop trains bound for Hampton Roads, Virginia. Once there, they loaded their gear on four troop ships and began their journey across the Atlantic and Mediterranean as part of a merchant convoy. The convoy made brief stops in North Africa and Italy, but, as noted in the aptly titled *Tuskegee Airmen*, the 332nd and its subordinate units "debarked in the ports of Bari, Taranto and Naples, Italy."[52]

Dr. Daniel Haulman, who chronicled the rich history of the Tuskegee Airmen through a detailed timeline of events, noted that the "[s]quadrons of the group traveled on other ships in the convoy with 301st spending their journey aboard the liberty ship *SS Clark*

---

[52] Stentiford, *Tuskegee Airmen*, 79.

Mills (HR-812).[53] Shipley explained that although he and the majority of the squadron became seasick, they were able to bide their time by playing cards, "hanging over the rails watching fish," going to the upper deck to view and participate in some impromptu boxing matches or by attending church services.

Upon their arrival in Italy in early February 1944, Shipley said, the first order of business was to prepare their temporary living quarters.

"The one thing I remember is that it was raining when we got off of the ship and me and James [Ross] had to put up our pup tents. We put our tent up on a hillside and forgot to trench around it," he continued, "and we ended up wet that night—all of our bedding was soaked! Needless to say, the next night we had a trench around the tent," he laughingly remarked.

Within days, the 301st Fighter Squadron moved to the aerodrome at the southwestern Italian community of Montecorvino Rovella. In 1943, Allied forces perceived Salerno's Montecorvino airfield as a necessary location to secure because "when captured, could sustain four fighter squadrons."[54] The airfield was eventually captured during Operation Avalanche in early September 1943 and then became an Allied airfield from where missions were launched in support of the remainder of the Italian campaign. Military leadership "believed that if Italy could be forced out of the war and if a sufficient portion of the country could be occupied by Allied forces, then air bases in the occupied territory could be used for strategic operations against Germany and her satellites." The airport at Montecorvino became part of this strategy and entered into reality in September 1943 (days prior to the arrival of the 301st Fighter Squadron) when it "was freed of enemy artillery fire … [and] immediately became the principal airdrome in the Salerno area."[55]

---

[53] The ship was named for Clark Mills, a self-taught American sculptor who was perhaps best known for his equestrian statue of Andrew Jackson that is located in Washington, D.C. According to the book *"A Careless Word … A Needless Sinking: A History of the Staggering Losses Suffered By the U.S. Merchant Marine, Both in Ships and in Personnel, During World War II,"* the S.S. Clark Mills was torpedoed and sank on March 9, 1944, but suffered no reported casualties.

[54] U.S. Army Center of Military History, *Naples-Foggia,* www.history.army.mil.

[55] Francis, *The Tuskegee Airmen: The Men Who Changed a Nation,* 71 & 78.

Early during their service in Italy, the 332nd Fighter Group was issued the P-39Q Airacobra. This photo provides a close-up of a variant of the P-39 in which the "nose cannon" that Shipley referred to is clearly visible. U.S. Air Force photograph.

It was here they joined up with both the 100th and 302nd Fighter Squadrons and began flying "Bell P-39 Airacobra fighters with the Twelfth Air Force, performing combat patrol over the Tyrennean Sea and strafing attacks in and around Cassino and Anzio, against the German army ..."[56] While there, many of the pilots and crewmembers began the process of familiarizing themselves with a plane slightly different than that which they had used in training.

---

[56] Sheppard, *Black Airmen in World War II*, www.bjmjr.net.

"The P-39s that we worked on seemed to be pretty good planes," said Shipley. "I remember that it had a cannon in the nose of the plane but a lot of pilots didn't seem to like it because they thought it was a little slow—they had become accustomed to the P-40s they had trained with."

U.S. Army Air Forces B-25 Mitchells—twine-engine bombers—fly in the vicinity of Mt. Vesuvius during its famed 1944 eruption. Not only did the eruption cause much turbulence for planes in the air, but the tons of volcanic ash that rained down caused a significant amount of damage to equipment on the ground. U.S. Air Force photograph.

The Bell P-39 Airacobra was one of the primary fighter aircraft used by the United States during the early stages of World War II and was essentially "a vehicle for a heavy-caliber cannon." The aircraft itself was essentially designed around the large nose cannon and the 332nd Fighter Group was equipped primarily with the P-39Q variant, of which four thousand nine hundred and five were produced for the Allied forces.[57]

Shipley added, "The weather was pretty good while we were over there, too, but there were some weeks during the winter when it would rain and snow and the planes would sit on the field because the conditions of the airfield wouldn't allow for safe landings or take-offs."

Though many of the mechanics were accustomed to working with the Allison engines in the P-39s, the fighter "was the first to have the engine installed in the center fuselage, behind the driver" and were considered by many pilots who served during the war to be "totally inadequate at high altitude."

While they refined their processes in working on the planes on the flight lines while at Montecorvino, Shipley explained that he

Three P-47 Thunderbolts flying in formation above the clouds. In addition to the P-47, the airmen of the 332nd Fighter Group went on to pilot an impressive list of planes including the P-39 Airacobra, P-40 Warhawk and the P-51 Mustang. U.S. Air Force photograph.

---

[57] Munson, *Fighters: 1939-1945*, 137-138.

and his fellow crew chiefs and members of the maintenance crews never questioned the importance of their work in keeping the aircraft operational.

"If you didn't do something right," he said, "they'd take your [sergeant] stripes[58] away in a minute. You didn't mess up and get away with it—you did your job because if you tried to slack or take a shortcut, it could get a pilot killed and that was never acceptable. Also, you had to account for every piece of equipment or tool that you used in doing your job; you didn't leave a screwdriver or a pair of pliers sitting in the seat of one of the planes," he admonished.

The 301st Squadron remained at Montecorvino while 100th Fighter Squadron moved to Capodichino, Italy in late February 1944 (the 302nd followed the 100th within less than a month's time). Although the squadrons of the group were now separated among different locations, the 301st received the unexpected opportunity to witness a historic event when the famed Mt. Vesuvius underwent its most recent eruption near Naples, Italy on March 15, 1944, and "layered Capodichino in fine ash, bringing pause to the aerial action from the base." [59]

The famed volcano "has experienced eight major eruptions in the last 17,000 years"—the last of which was in 1944—"and is the only active volcano in mainland Europe." It is perhaps best known for its eruption in 79 AD that destroyed the Roman cities of Pompeii and Herculaneum.[60]

"Mt. Vesuvius was really something to see—it was one of those places that I remembered reading about back when we were in school but it was one of those places that I never imagined I would have gotten the chance to see in person," he said. "When it erupted, the smoke and ashes kept puffing up and blowing over our camp." He continued: "It caused us some problems because those hot ashes would end up falling down onto the planes and burning spots in the canopies ... leaving behind a little scar. When the pilots were flying, they would be looking at the spots and not be able to tell whether it was an enemy plane approaching or just one of these burn spots. We

---

[58] Shipley is referring to the stripes associated with various enlisted ranks. To have a stripe "taken away" means that a military member was demoted.
[59] Bucholtz, *332nd Fighter Group*, 38.
[60] Ball, *Mt. Vesuvius*, www.geology.com.

ended up changing several canopies because of this. Also," he concluded, "you'd be busy doing some kind of work and feel something hot kind of burning on your shoulder or back ... and it was one of the ashes that had fallen out of the sky."

In mid-April 1944, the 301st joined rest of the 332nd Fighter Group at the airfield in Capodichino[61] where Shipley and the other mechanics continued their dedicated efforts of keeping all of the planes running smoothly and in the air supporting missions. Within the next few weeks, Air Force records indicate, the squadron began receiving new planes, the P-47 Thunderbolt, to replace some of their P-39Qs. The first operation-level P-47B was officially handed over to the U.S. Army on May 26, 1942" and "was produced more than any other fighter during the war." The aircraft was powered by a Pratt & Whitney R2800 Double Wasp, 18 cylinder engine and armed with eight wing mounted Browning .50 caliber machine guns which could deliver 13 pounds of lead per second.[62]

The transition to the P-47 aircraft highlighted the support the men of the 332nd Fighter Group did receive from certain higher level military authorities, such as General Ira C. Eaker, who was at the time serving as air commander-in-chief of the Mediterranean Allied Air Forces with both the Twelfth and Fifteenth Air Forces under his command. In a letter to Major General Barney M. Giles on March 6, 1944, he expressed his desire to have the 332nd Fighter Group equipped with the P-47s after a demonstration of their performance with the Twelfth Air Force and further noted that, should they be issued the P-47s, "Colonel Davis and his colored pilots are most enthusiastic to undertake the program and I am confident that they will do a good job."[63]

---

[61] Now the Naples Airport (also known as Capodichino Airport), the airfield in Capodichino was established during World War I to help defend the community of Naples against attacks from Austro Hungarian and German aircraft. During the Second World War, it was used by the 12th Air Force as a combat airfield.
[62] Military Factory, *Republic P-47 Thunderbolt Fighter*, www.militaryfactory.com.

[63] Lee, *The Employment of Negro Troops*, 518.

"Not long after we got to Italy, most of the missions that our pilots were doing involved flying up and down the coast looking for enemy planes, but at that time they weren't encountering a whole lot of enemy planes," Shipley said. "They were also flying some harbor patrols and air cover for convoys—nothing that really put them in harm's way or in situations where they would encounter any real threats."

He added, "Some of the places and dates might be just a little foggy to me, but I think it was while we were in Capodichino," Shipley recalled, "that they talked about sending me to somewhere in Africa to work specifically on carburetors. It was not something that I asked to do but fortunately I didn't have to go," he said. As Shipley noted, such duty would have moved him away from the group of soldiers with whom he had trained and come to recognize as friends during the previous months.

Their stay in Capodichino—although brief—brought with it many disturbing experiences, such as the attack on the airfield that occurred one evening in late April 1944. While Shipley and the other members of the ground crews slept in their tents to rest up for the coming day's flight preparations, the anti-aircraft guns that were situated around the field and manned by British troops began to explode as they sent countless rounds of ordnance into the sky; the raucous thunder created by the projectiles when bursting forth from the barrels jolted everyone from their peaceful slumbers.

"I don't know if it was only a single German plane or several because I was sleeping when this all went down and it all happened so quickly," Shipley recalled. "What I do remember that all of us bolted out of our tents to see what was going on and it looked like a bomb had been dropped on the airfield; many of the planes were smoking and in flames. Several of the planes had been destroyed including the one that I worked on. The next day our pilots brought in a bunch of new planes and we had to work to get them all ready to head out on missions," which, he added, included performing such necessary preparatory tasks as "tuning the engines, checking the coolant and removing any water in the gas lines."

Although Shipley was never informed as to the number of aircraft that were disabled or destroyed during the attack on the airfield, his personal estimate that   between forty-five to fifty planes received some form of damage.

The pilots' engagement in "flying air patrols over Naples Harbor and the Mediterranean Sea"[64] would soon come to an end when the 332nd Fighter Group made another move that would allow them to be more involved in the war effort. This next assignment provided the opportunity to depart the daily encounters which had hitherto been less than exhilarating for the pilots and support crew; allowing them to become engaged in the combat operations for which they had trained for nearly the past two years.

May 1944 brought with it not only a transfer of the 332nd Fighter Group from the Twelfth Air Force to the Fifteenth Air Force, but also a demonstration of the temporary nature of their duty locations during a period of war when the airmen were told to pack up their gear and then boarded trucks to convoy to the airfield at Ramitelli, Italy[65]—the site that would serve as their home for the remainder of the war.

---

[64] The Tuskegee Airmen National Historical Museum, *Who Were They?*, www.tuskegeemuseum.org.
[65] The temporary airfield that once existed at Ramitelli was dismantled after the war and the area has been returned to agricultural uses.

Chapter 4
Arrival in Ramitelli

"You are fighting men now. You have made the team. Your future, good or bad, will depend largely on how determined you are not to give satisfaction to those who would like to see you fail." –Col. Noel F. Parrish

"When we got [to Ramitelli], the base was pretty much already set up for us to fall in on," Shipley explained. "The engineers were still completing the work on the one airstrip on the base and it was basically just a dirt road that was covered with a type of steel mat."

During World War II, "The U.S. military began using pierced steel planks (PSP) mats" that had the ability "to handle minor surface deficiencies but generally needed a stabilized sub grade to function efficiently. Typical PSP matting was 10ft x 16" and made of hardened steel."[66] In the years following World War II, the mats eventually fell into disuse as the heavier wheel loads of the

---

[66] Signature Aviation Matting, *A History of Landing Mats*, www.signatureaviationmatting.com.

emerging jet aircraft were too great and required a different, more solid type of landing surface.

Constructed by the U.S. Army Corps of Engineers in early 1944, the air base at Ramitelli had a single runway with a few farm houses and structures around the airfield that had been repurposed to serve as operations centers. The men of the 301st Fighter Squadron quickly began to assimilate into their new work environment and began to set up their temporary homes inside tents on the new airbase while they watched the activity around the field build to a frenetic crescendo.

The air field at Ramitelli was considered part of the Foggia Airfield Complex—a network "of about 30 airfields on the Tavoliere plain around Foggia, Apulia, Italy." Many of these airfields "had already been of strategic importance during World War I, but it became even more so during the Albanian and Greek campaigns of 1940-1941," and once they were recaptured, were repaired by the Army Corps of Engineers and used as bases for Allied aircraft.[67]

"I believe there were six of us that stayed in the tent[68]—we were all mechanics," he stated. "The sides of the tents were made of pretty flimsy canvas and wouldn't hold heat very well so what we decided to do was take the wood from the crates that the gas tanks for the planes came in and then used them to build walls around the outside of the tent." Hesitating, he added, "It might not have been the prettiest setup, but we used what he had available and it really made it a lot easier for us to heat the tents."

As Shipley explained, the entire airbase was essentially built around the landing strip with all the planes situated on either side of the airfield and positioned so to be able to take-off on a short notice. "The mechanics worked outside and we stayed near our plane all of the time," he said. "We kept all of our tools in a toolbox and took them back to our tents with us when we were done working on the planes. Also," he continued, "we all had an assigned area just off the runway where the airplane we were assigned to would park when it wasn't out on a mission and that's where you did your maintenance

---

[67] Abandoned, Forgotten & Little Known Airfields in Europe, *Foggia Airfield Complex*, www.forgottenairfiels.com.

[68] The men of the 332nd were no longer staying the aforementioned "pup tents," they now set up their homes in larger, more spacious canvas tents.

work. You didn't want to leave your plane for too long because parts were sometimes difficult to acquire and if another mechanic needed something for his plane, then the part he needed might just disappear off your plane," he smiled.

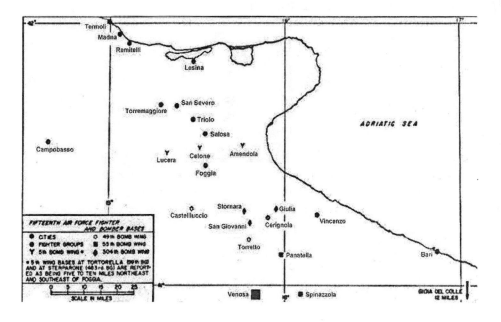

This map shows the location of Fifteenth Air Force Air Fields located around Italy during the Second World War. Ramitelli, which was the final location where Shipley served with the 332nd Fighter Group, is located on the upper left section of the map. United States Air Force photograph

When the pilots came back from flying their missions, Shipley and the other mechanics would work diligently to ensure their pilot would be able to step into his plane the next day and fly without worries or concerns regarding the aircraft's performance. Inspections, he explained, were critical because they helped identify potential issues before they became a major safety concern.

"You had to check all of the cables—like the ones that controlled the rudders," he said. "They had to have the correct tension and you made sure they weren't frayed and that none of the pulleys were cracked. If they were," he continued, "then you would remove them and install a new one. Some of the other things we were doing were to change the spark plugs or check and change the oil; basically, we made sure everything was in good shape.

The uniforms the mechanics wore on a daily basis, the veteran recalled, consisted of a khaki-style shirt that they tucked into pants of identical material and color.

"When we were on the flight line, we wore a hat that was similar to a ball cap. Most of the time, you would see the mechanics with the bill of the hat folded up so that they could see what they were working on better. We had a different kind of hat that we wore on other occasions, like whenever we went to town or something like that."

On the field opposite of where Shipley remained with his plane was a shop—an "actual building, not a tent"—that he describes as being used for "more involved maintenance," such as engine repairs that could not be performed by the mechanics while the plane they supported was parked on the side of the airstrip.

In early June 1944, the 332nd Fighter Group was given their first bomber escort responsibility when sent to provide aerial protection for the B-17s of the 5th Bombardment Wing on a mission to Pola, Italy. Not only did his event afford the black airmen the opportunity to demonstrate to the white bomber pilots their courage under hostile fire, but also highlighted their keen abilities in protecting the bulky and slow bombers from the machine guns of German aircraft.

***

The 332nd, like most military organizations during World War II, would lose a number of lives attributable to direct combat but, as Shipley recalls, there were also deaths that were a result of accident and, which demonstrated the many dangers that would remain a persistent threat to their safety. One such event unfolded on June 2, 1944, while the pilots and ground crews of the 301st and 302nd Fighter Squadrons prepared to dispatch their planes on one another of their many training missions.

"It was really busy on the airstrip and all the planes were taking off for a mission—one after another in rapid succession," he said. "One of the planes—well, I'm not absolutely certain exactly how it all unfolded—but it had just lifted off of the runway and the engine seized up or something, and the plane just slammed to the ground. The engine caught fire and the pilot breathed a bunch of smoke and flames from the engine while he was scrambling to get out of the cockpit." Somberly, Shipley noted, "The pilot managed to get the canopy open and exited the aircraft, but then took only a couple of steps and fell to the ground. He was dead from all of the nasty stuff he breathed into his lungs."

Pictured are pilots of the 332nd Fighter Group while stationed at the airbase in Ramitelli. From left: Lt. Dempsey W. Morgan, Lt. Carroll S. Woods, Lt. Robert H. Nelron, Jr., Captain Andrew D. Turner, and Lt. Clarence P. Lester. Note the pierced steel planks in the foreground that Shipley noted were used to cover the landing strip. U.S. Air Force photograph.

The book *Tuskegee Airmen: An Illustrated History, 1939-1949* confirms that that the 302nd was participating in a training mission on the date of the horrific incident and identifies the pilot killed as 2nd Lt. Elmer Taylor[69]—a native of Pennsylvania.

But this was not the end of the day's tragedy, as Shipley recalls looking down the runway and seeing a large cloud of smoke emanating from site of the plane's accident, at which point Master Sergeant William Harris,[70] line chief with the 332nd Fighter Group, ran down the runway to determine the extent of the damage to the disabled aircraft and to assist the pilot.

"The planes had a mission they had to get to and they just kept going … they kept taking off one right after another because you couldn't let anything stop you from performing your mission," said Shipley.

"When Harris got near the area where the plane had slammed down onto the runway, one of the fighters that was lifting off banked to the left to avoid the black smoke that was still rising and blocking his view, believing that he had cleared Harris [who was standing on the ground]."

---

[69] Elmer W. Taylor was born in Pennsylvania in 1918. According to newspaper records, he was a junior at Virginia State College when he enlisted and later appointed a cadet in the Air Force, receiving his lieutenant's commission in 1943. At the time of his death on June 2, 1944, Taylor was 26 years old and had been overseas five months and completed thirty five missions. His body was initially buried overseas but was returned to Pennsylvania and interred in Homewood Cemetery in Pittsburgh on April 9, 1949. April 7, 1949 edition of *The Pittsburgh Press*.
[70] William M. Harris was born in Miami, Ohio on November 21, 1920. His body appears to have been initially interred in Italy on June 2, 1944, but according to the *Find A Grave* website, his remains were returned to his native Miami County, Ohio and interred in Forest Hill Cemetery on December 15, 1948. Find A Grave, *William M. Harris.* www.findagrave.com.

Master Sergeant William M. Harris, far right, is pictured in front of a P-51 Mustang with a group of soldiers from the ground crew of the 332nd Fighter Group while stationed at Ramitelli, Italy. Harris served as a line chief for the flight line was killed during an accident on the airfield on June 2, 1944. Notice the khaki-style uniforms Shipley referenced, I addition to the hats with the bills folded up. **Courtesy of James Shipley.**

Sadly, as Shipley somberly explained, "Since the plane was just taking off, the landing gear was still down. One of the small doors that close when the wheel retracts after the plane was in the air struck Harris in the head and killed him." With a pause, he concluded, "The pilot didn't know that he had accidentally killed Harris and they waited until after he returned from his mission to tell him; they wanted him to be focused on doing his job and not worrying about what had just happened on the runway."

While reflecting on the crash and the loss of two comrades, Shipley affirms that although he would not consider himself to have been a close friend of Harris, he knew that he was a "good guy" who worked diligently to keep the group's aircraft operational and ready to head out on missions.

"As the line chief, he would frequently come down the flight line to see if you were having any troubles with your plane and if you needed help, he would see that you got it. He was always busy and you could see him running up and down the entire flight line trying to take care of whatever work needed to be done so that our missions weren't' delayed."

***

The stellar performance of the pilots in the air was setting records and making history while the crews on the airfield were committed to keeping the planes to which they were assigned in peak condition. It was critical duty, they quickly discovered, since the Tuskegee pilots and their assigned aircraft had to be prepared to engage the lethal German aircraft they would encounter, including variants of fighters such as the Messerschmitt Bf 109s[71] and Focke-Wulf Fw-190s.[72]

"It always seemed like we were on the move … we were very busy," he said. "I remember times when some of the other mechanics had planes that would come back from the strafing runs and they had flown at such a low altitude during the mission that enemy soldiers on the ground had shot at them from below and put holes in the wings. It always seemed like certain materials and spare parts were often very hard to come by so we ended up using the aluminum from old beer cans [that were purchased at the Post Exchange] to patch the holes in the wings. Other times, "he

---

[71] Also known as the ME-109, the Messerschmitt Bf 109 "became the most widely produced, the most respected and the most varied Luftwaffe fighter." Later models of this aircraft provided for much greater speeds and horsepower than those available in many American planes—such as that seen by the Bf-109 G (or "Gustav). This plane, which was introduced in early 1942, was equipped with a 1,450 horsepower Daimler Benz engine, was fitted with a pressurized cockpit, and armed with a 20mm cannon and two 7.9mm machine guns. Ace Pilots, *Messerschmitt Bf 109*, www.acepilots.com.

[72] The Focke-Wulf Fw 190 was more heavily armed that its contemporary, the British Spitfire, "carrying four 20 mm cannons in addition to two 13 mm machine guns." Additionally, because of the aircraft's high kill rate, it earned the title of "Butcher Bird." Flying Heritage Collection, *Focke-Wulfe Fw 190*, www.flyingheritage.com.

continued, "there were much bigger holes to patch, especially when the pilots got into flak.

With a grin, he added, "There was no use complaining because it wouldn't change anything. You just had to use whatever you could get your hands on and be creative at times if you wanted to keep everything running smoothly."

While the planes were out on a mission, Shipley and the members of the ground crews would often have several hours to relax and unwind. Many of the enlisted soldiers would gather in a specific tent to play cards or other types of games to bide the time until the planes made their return.

"There were a lot of guys that enjoyed playing card games like Whist or Bridge, but I never was a card player so I would lie around and read books or something," Shipley said. "Other times, there was a guy who played guitar that would come over and hang out in our tent and play some songs and sing for us. There were even occasions when we would have baseball games to keep us occupied."

According to Shipley, when he first arrived at Ramitelli, there was an officers' club but not an enlisted club. However, he noted that later in his stay at the Italian airfield a club for enlisted service members was established, such as the one pictured in this photograph. Courtesy of James Shipley

Initially, said Shipley, the officers of the 332nd Fighter Group established an officers' club at which they could spend their downtime; however, it was many months into their stay at Ramitelli before a club was built for the enlisted personnel.

"Sometimes the pilots would come by our tents and visit but they mostly kept to themselves," he said. "It wasn't that they thought they were any better than us, you just kind of stuck with people that had similar duties and rank."

The ground crews often knew when the planes were scheduled to return from their missions, but if they were making an early return, they could hear them from a distance and would make their way back to their assigned area along the airfield to meet the planes and begin their preparations for the next day of missions. On occasion, Shipley clearly recalled, the pilots were so exhausted from their missions that they would have the crew chief crawl in the cockpit and taxi the plane back to the its parking position along the airstrip runway. As the crew chief, Shipley would then perform any necessary maintenance procedures on his aircraft and then coordinate the specialists who would come perform their specific support functions.

"There were members of the crew who were armor guys and they would reload the plane with ammunition and check the guns, making sure they were clean," Shipley said. "There were many other specialists like instrument guys," he added. "If there was an instrument or a gauge that didn't seem like it was working properly—or quit working all together—it was their job to replace it. There were also guys that would come along to check the cameras[73] and those that came down the flight line and refueled all of the planes, too."

Another specialty outside of the ground crew that was considered by most to be of the greatest importance was the cooks. The food, Shipley laughingly recalled, was often the "basic Army type" about which the soldiers would often "put up a big fuss about how bad they thought it tasted"; however, he added with a grin, "it

---

[73] Shipley is referring to gun cameras, which were installed on many different types of aircraft during World War II. The ones placed on the fighter of the 332nd were essentially activated when the aircrafts' weapons began firing and were commonly used to record the number of confirmed "kills" by the pilot.

seemed like all of the soldiers that I knew came out of the Army a little heavier than they were when they went in, so they definitely had no problems getting enough to eat."

He continued, "The chow was something we often looked forward to and they had a big tent [on Ramitelli Air Base] set up with a bunch of tables and chairs inside. For breakfast we could get pancakes and sometimes they would have sausage and oatmeal; lunch might be stew or something like that; and dinner might be fried chicken or some type of meat. All in all, I really didn't think the food was all that bad."

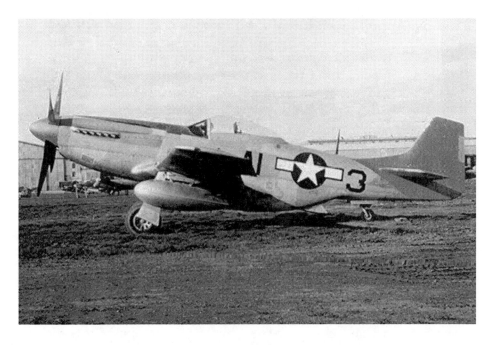

The P-51 Mustang was considered the favorite aircraft among the pilots of the 332nd. While the group was stationed at Ramitelli, they decided they needed a paint scheme for the tail sections of their planes so that they would be recognizable to the gunners on the bombers they were escorting. As the story goes, the only available paint was bright red signal paint, which soon led to the group's designation as "Red Tails." U.S. Air Force Photograph

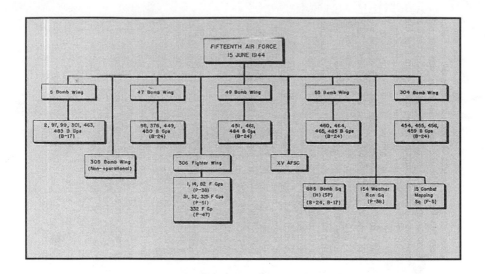

This organizational chart shows the structure of the Fifteenth Air Force as of June 15, 1944, several weeks after the 332nd Fighter Group move to the airfield at Ramitelli and shortly their reassignment from the Twelfth Air Force. U.S. Air Force photograph.

Late June and early July 1944 brought two significant changes to Ramitelli—the transfer of the 99th Fighter Squadron[74] to the base and the much welcomed arrival of the first P-51 Mustangs—the planes that would become the signature aircraft for the Tuskegee Airmen.

The Mustangs made their entry into service with the United States military in March 1942 as the P-51A model and its delay in reaching the 332nd Fighter Group more than two years later may have been a form of blessing. By the time Shipley and his fellow Tuskegee Airmen received the aircraft, it had undergone several improvements and changes. The Mustangs were initially equipped with an Allison engine but "lacked power at high altitudes." Additionally, the canopies on the early models had "braces that blocked a pilot's rear vision."[75]

---

[74] Although the 99th Fighter Squadron had been assigned to the 332nd Fighter Group since May 1, 1944, they had spent the previous two months prior to their arrival at Ramitelli flying combat missions while attached to other fighter groups throughout Italy.
[75] Zuchora-Walske, *The Tuskegee Airmen*, 12-13.

Many of these shortcomings were soon corrected when the P-51D was re-equipped with the British-designed "Merlin" engine manufactured by Rolls-Royce. Not only would the new engine help improve the plane's performance at higher altitudes "thanks to its "two-stage, two-speed supercharger,"[76] it would also allow for greater fuel efficiency and, when combined with its external fuel tanks, would provide the aircraft with a range of more than 1,000 miles—an important characteristic since many of the bombing campaigns later in the war required pilots to fly greater distances. Furthermore, the P-51D boasted a "transparent plastic bubble canopy, or cockpit enclosure, allowing the pilot to see clearly in all directions."[77]

Shipley noted, "Any time you got a new plane, like the P-51, you didn't really get any training or classes; instead, you just kind of fell into it and learned how to work on it. They didn't seem to be too much different than the previous planes we had worked on—it was just another engine to us," he grinned. "They furnished all of the tools that we needed to support the aircraft and it was our job to make sure we kept the planes in the air."

It was not long after the arrival of the high-performance P-51s, Shipley recalled, that a decision was made within the 332nd Fighter Group that would forever secure their designation as "Red Tails."

"There were some problems with our fighters coming in too quickly when they were assigned to escort a group of bombers, and occasionally the bomber gunners would start firing at our guys because they couldn't distinguish our planes from those of the Germans until they got a little closer."

Other squadrons, he stated, were using different paint schemes on the tails of their planes to make them more recognizable to the pilots of the bombers they were escorting—such as a yellow stripe or a checkerboard pattern. Soon, Shipley added, the 332nd decided upon paint scheme specific to their squadron—which,

[76] Dorr, *P-51 Mustang's Switch to Merlin Engine,* www.defensemedianetwork.com.
[77] Zuchora-Walske, *The Tuskegee Airmen,* 13.

interestingly enough, was more the result of availability rather than design.

"Some of the guys found some bright red signal paint because that was all that was really available at the time ... they couldn't find anything else," Shipley recalled. "So we took what we could get and used it to paint the tails of the planes red and, of course, I guess the rest is history," he laughed.

There were some initial concerns expressed, Shipley said, such as those who questioned if the bright red tails would make the 332nd planes stand out against the backdrop of the sky, making them easier targets for the German fighters. But as noted in *Black Knights*, the coloring on the tails of their planes "made no difference to the German gunners on the ground, since they saw only silhouettes." Additionally, the authors further discussed, the color not only made the airmen more recognizable to the bombers they were escorting, but it also made it easier for the airmen to recognize their fellow pilots "in the thick of a dogfight"[78] when the speed of battle made other planes seem like an indistinguishable blur.

"We had painters that painted all of the planes and it sure was a loud color, alright!" Shipley exclaimed. "But we all liked it."

With their tails serving as a bright beacon in the sky, Shipley bears a wide grin when he recalls hearing the story of how the bomber pilots soon began to recognize the 332nd because of the tails of the their planes in addition to the incredulity the new paint scheme caused.

"Of course, those bomber pilots soon figured out that our planes were the ones escorting them on the trips and about the first time we shot down some German planes while protecting them, they really had a hard time believing what we had done," he said. "They couldn't believe that they had been so well protected by black pilots."

---

[78] Homan & Reilly, *Black Knights*, 130.

Chapter 5

The Mission Continues ...

"Discriminatory practices are morally wrong wherever they occur—they are especially inequitable and iniquitous when they inconvenience and embarrass those serving in the Armed Services and their families." –Pres. John F. Kennedy

Shipley and the dedicated members of the ground crews continued to toil long hours, and oftentimes into the early hours of morning, maintaining the planes of the squadron. Oftentimes, the veteran explained, the mechanics and support personnel had to be prepared to address a variety of mechanical issues that unfolded. In some instances, the planes were in the air during a mission when problems arose, thus requiring the use of peculiar means by which to prevent accidents and get the pilots back on the ground for necessary repairs on their aircraft.

"I must say, I was pretty fortunate the entire time that I was stationed in Italy because the aircraft I worked on never had any major problems like some of the other mechanics did," he said. "There was never a time that I had to change a tire or pull a wheel because they were retracted while the plane was in the air [during the mission] and didn't get much wear on the landings unless the pilot was a little hard on the brakes," he laughed. "But you always checked the tires to make sure they were still in good condition and some of them did have to be changed out on some of the other planes, though. There were also those who said there were problems getting parts as well; but I never had too many issues getting the parts I needed—then again, I didn't have any serious problems to contend with, either."

When the pilots returned from their missions, Shipley explained, the mechanics and ground crew would often work around the clock to prepare the planes for the next day's mission. Pictured above is a member of the 332nd Fighter Group's ground crew fueling one of the P-51s at the airfield in Ramitelli. Courtesy of James Shipley

There were some situations, he further explained, when the landing gear was lowered in preparation for a pilot's landing; however, there was the infrequent circumstance when the gear would fail to "lock" into position and thus posed a serious safety concern for both the pilot and the crews on the ground awaiting their return.

"The pilots had a gauge inside the cockpit of the plane—at least on the P-51s—that would indicate whether or not the wheels were locked into the proper position for landing," he explained. "If the wheels didn't lock out like they were supposed to do, the pilots would have to shake the plane back and forth. The motion from the rocking the plane [left to right] would then force them to lock into position and the pilots could then land safely. It was just one of those things that you somehow figured out along the way," said the former mechanic while explaining one of the integral lessons he received at Ramitelli.

As was the case with many pieces of military equipment used in combat throughout the Second World War—including everything from tanks and ships to various types of aircraft—many of the men found a level of solace while living and working in a combat environment by naming some of their vehicles and aircraft, a practice that often served as a reminder of the loved ones that were anxiously awaiting their return back to the states.

"There was one of the planes that I took care of that had been given the name *Ms. Jackson*," Shipley recalled. "There was a picture of a girl in a bikini painted on the plane right beside the name—like there was on so many of the aircraft," he sheepishly grinned. "One of the armor guys gave the plane that name but I never really knew if it was named for his wife, girlfriend or some woman that he was in love with."

Shipley's time served in Ramitelli also placed him in close proximity with some of the Tuskegee Airmen that would acquire a virtual legendary status in the annals of World War II history, which included such renowned pilots as Charles Edward McGee.

Born in Cleveland, Ohio, McGee was raised by his father (his mother passed away giving birth to McGee's sister). Since his father did not have the money to pay for McGee's college, the future aviator worked briefly for the Civilian Conservation Corps before enrolling at the University of Illinois in 1940, where he became an engineering student and participated in the Reserve Officer Training Program. After the Japanese attack on Pearl Harbor, McGee "heard the army was recruiting to train colored soldiers as mechanics at nearby Chanute Field, for the expected colored soldiers' flight program." The aspiring airman applied for a pilot's slot, took the applicable examination and, on October 19, 1942 (two days after wedding his fiancée), "received his orders and soon was at Tuskegee

Army Air Field in Alabama to begin rigorous flight training with his fellow black cadets."

Graduating from flight school on June 30, 1943, McGee joined Shipley and the other soldiers and airmen of the 332nd Fighter Group as they deployed to Italy, where he began flying missions in a P-39 Airacobra, progressed to the P-47 Thunderbolt and finally the P-51 Mustang. By November 1944, he had completed 136 missions and was credited with downing a Focke-Wulfe 190.[79]

"McGee's plane sat right across the runway from me [at Ramitelli]," Shipley said. "Of course, you'd occasionally see each other around and we would talk some, but pilots tended to go their own way and we would go ours," he added. "When the pilots hit the ground, they were focused on getting ready to take off on their mission and didn't have time to do a lot of visiting."

Following his return to the states, McGee served as a twin-engine aircraft instructor at Tuskegee and later completed several other stateside assignments. In 1950, he became the base operations officer at Clark Field in the Philippines and during the Korean War flew 100 missions with the 67th Fighter Bomber Squadron while operating out of an air base in Pusan. In the ensuing years, he went on to serve in assignments of increasing responsibility and rank and was promoted to lieutenant colonel in 1959. During the Vietnam War he flew 172 missions in the RF-4C Phantom (photo-reconnaissance aircraft) and was promoted to the rank of colonel in 1969. In 1972, he entered his final duty assignment as commander of the 1840th Air Base Wing at Richards-Gebaur[80] south of Kansas City, Missouri, and retired the following year with thirty years of service to his credit and an impressive 6,308 flying hours.

---

[79] The National Aviation Hall of Fame, *Charles Edward McGee*, www.nationalaviation.org.
[80] Richards-Gebaur Air Force Base was an 1,362 acre air base and airfield that operated from 1941 to 2001 at Belton, Missouri. It was built in 1941 by Kansas City and named Grandview Airport. In 1955, the property was transferred to the Air Force and became Grandview Air Force Base. It was named Richards-Gebaur in 1957 in honor of Kansas City residents John Francisco Richards II (an airman killed in World War II) and Arthur William Gebauer Jr. (an airman killed during the Korean War). The Air Force deactivated the base in 1976 and the property was then deeded back to Kansas City in 1985.

Shipley came into contact with many notable pilots while stationed at Tuskegee, which included Charles McGee. While a member of the Red Tails, McGee flew 136 missions and later flew in combat during both the Korean and Vietnam Wars. Courtesy of Museum of Military History.

The military, as seemed to be the case for many of the Tuskegee Airmen, interrupted McGee's pursuit of a college degree and he enrolled at Columbia College in Kansas City, earning his degree in 1978 at the age of fifty-eight. He would later serve as the vice president of a real estate holding company and also as the manager of the Kansas City Downtown Airport. In 2011, he was inducted to the National Aviation Hall of Fame in Dayton, Ohio. As noted by Shipley, McGee has also remained active in sharing his story of his service as a member of the 332nd Fighter Group with school groups and other interested organizations and individuals, and continues to serve as a testament to the ideals of freedom and equality for which he and his fellow "Red Tails" fought.

Mechanics such as Shipley would often support more than one pilot during the time they spent overseas since the aviators often rotated back to the states after "flying an average of between seventy and eighty missions, while their white counterparts returned home after only fifty missions."[81]

"The first pilot I worked with was [Willie] Hunter,[82]" said Shipley. "He was very good at what he did and finally flew enough missions that he was able to return back to the United States. The second pilot I was assigned to support was a guy with the last name of Smith ... and I don't really remember what his first name was, but I think he was from somewhere in the South," he added.

The final pilot for whom he would maintain his aircraft in peak operational condition was Harry T. Stewart, Jr.,[83] who would not only become one of the most decorated of the Tuskegee Airmen, but has remained a close friend of Shipley's.

Born July 24, 1924, a biography on the website of the Jackson County, Michigan[84] notes that Stewart was raised in New

---

[81] Homan & Reilly, *Black Knights*, 168.

[82] Records accessed from the National Archives denote that Willie Sheappard Hunter was born in 1921 and enlisted in the U.S. Army Air Forces on October 20, 1942 at Tuskegee, Alabama. A listing of pilot graduates accessed through the website of Tuskegee University show that Hunter, a native of Albany Georgia, graduated in Class 43-F-SE at Tuskegee Flight School on June 30, 1943 at the rank of second lieutenant. According to the Find A Grave website, the Tuskegee pilot is buried in Riverside Cemetery at Albany, Georgia. Tuskegee University, *Tuskegee Airmen Pilot Listing*, www.tuskegee.edu.

[83] Harry T. Stewart, Jr., remained in the Air Force Reserve after receiving his discharge in 1950, eventually rising to the rank of lieutenant colonel. After the war he earned a bachelor's degree in mechanical engineering by attending evening classes and New York University and later became vice president of ANR Pipeline Company—a major natural gas consortium—before retiring. As of the publication of this book, he resides in Bloomfield Hills, Michigan. Gathering of Eagles Foundation, *Lieutenant Colonel Harry Stewart*, www.goefoudation.org.

[84] Jackson County Government, *Biography of Harry T. Stewart, Jr.*, www.co.jackson.mi..us.

York where he enlisted in the U.S. Army Air Corps as an aviation cadet during the Second World War. The aspiring aviator went on to complete his flight training at Tuskegee Army Air Field and earned his pilot wings and commission as a second lieutenant. Stewart then underwent combat fighter training to acquire his proficiency in both the P-40 and P-47 aircraft before he was sent to Italy with the 332nd Fighter Group, eventually receiving assignment to Ramitelli where he began flying the P-51 and was soon introduced to his new crew chief and mechanic, James Shipley.

***

Stewart explained during a 2016 telephone interview that while growing up in New York City, "equality was more evident and much more observed than it was in many other places in the United States."

Though his story has been well chronicled in several publications, Stewart noted the path that led him to Ramitelli and his eventual friendship with Shipley began in his early years and was the result of his burgeoning interest in aviation.

"By the time I was nineteen, I was a pilot," he said. "I couldn't even drive a car but I could fly," he chuckled. "In New York City, you had the subway and all of the mass transit systems, so my family really didn't need a car and there wasn't much need for me to drive, either."

When his stateside training as a pilot with the Tuskegee Airmen was completed in late 1944, Stewart boarded a troop ship that eventually took him to Italy, where he disembarked at the southern Italian port city of Taranto. Shortly following his arrival, he was "taken by the British on a truck from Naples and driven up to Ramitelli along the Adriatic Coast," recalled the former airman.

He further described his arrival overseas: "When we finally reached Ramitelli (in December 1944), it was two in the morning, I believe. I remember that it was raining and cold … not a good first impression at all." He added, "Then, they awakened the supply officer and he came and issued us some tent poles, canvas, cots, sleeping bags and such, and then pointed out a spot where we could set everything up. It was about dawn before we had everything ready and finally laid down for some sleep."

The morning following their arrival, Stewart and the remainder of the newly arrived airmen were taken down to the flight line by the operations officer, at which time each pilot was shown their spot on the flight line, the plane they would soon be piloting and were introduced to the crew chief for their respective aircraft.

Harry T. Stewart Jr., foreground, is pictured on April 1, 1945 after returning from an escort mission. Stewart is holding up three fingers to indicate that he shot down three Me-109s (an accomplishment that earned him a Distinguished Flying Cross); however, his jubilance was tempered by the reality that two of his fellow "Red Tail" pilots lost their lives during the same engagement with German fighters. Pictured behind Stewart is his crew chief, Jim Shipley. Courtesy of James Shipley.

"Jim [Shipley] was standing by his plane when I first met him," said Stewart. "I didn't want to ask 'Is this my aircraft?' because he might retort with 'No, this is my aircraft!'"

The same day, Stewart and several of the other new pilots were provided with an instruction manual on the P-51 Mustang and they spent much of the day reading and absorbing all the information they could with regard to the specifics of an airplane they had yet to operate. (Previous to his arrival at Ramitelli, Stewart had taken combat fighter training in both the P-40 and P-47 airplanes.)

"After reviewing the manual, the next day we were given a blindfold check to see if we could point out the instruments and other appurtenances of the aircraft," Stewart recalled. "Then," he continued, "we each took our own plane off and landed it and that was our indoctrination to begin flying missions," he affirmed. "It wasn't very long before we began escorting bombers on missions that could last four to six and a half hours."

Though he had already experienced piloting earlier models of fighter aircraft prior to his arrival in Italy, Stewart noted that his introduction to the P-51 was a moment he still views as quite memorable.

"While we were at Ramitelli, we had three models of P-51s that we operated—the B, C, and D models. The plane was faster ... smoother," he said. "The control of the aircraft was very sensitive and it had a good turning radius and a lot of firepower."

He soon began a frenetic schedule of bomber escorts and strafing missions; however, this did not conceal from him the importance of the ground crews in maintaining the planes' performance under what could be considered less than ideal conditions.

"It was definitely a pilot/crew chief relationship," said Stewart "The safety and preparation of the plane was entirely in the hands of Jim. The crew chief is the person that has overall control of the maintenance of the aircraft and can say whether the plane is going anywhere or if it isn't." He added, "The crew chief specialized in the engine and other components of the aircraft but he also had an assistant crew chief, armament chief, instrument chief and people that specialized in other areas such as electronics and radios."

As the war progressed, so did the length of the pilots' missions, as Stewart recalls making a 1,600-mile round trip to Berlin to escort bombers toward the latter part of the war in Europe. All the while, Shipley devoted his efforts to preserving the performance capabilities of the aircraft despite the wear and tear of combat operations.

"There was one day, I remember, that we didn't fly a mission—it was very cold, muddy and generally uncomfortable," Stewart said. "For some reason, I decided to go down to the flight line and [Shipley] was dropping the coolant tank from the plane. He was blowing on his fingers to try and keep them warm because he couldn't wear gloves since he needed to be able to remove bolts and such. That was one of many instances that proved to me the dedication he had for the safety and condition of the aircraft."

When told about Stewart's reflections, Shipley responded, "Yes, I remember that he came down to the flight line and asked if me if he could help but I told him that I could handle it. I guess he just felt sorry for me," the former crew chief laughed.

Pausing, Stewart concluded, "Without [Shipley's] shepherding and maintaining the plane—the tender care he gave it—I very possibly may not have been here to speak to you about it."

In May 1949, four years after his service as a Red Tail, Stewart was able to demonstrate many of the aerial performance lessons he had acquired during combat when participating in a ten-day competition known as the "William Tell" National Gunnery meet at Las Vegas Air Force Base (now Nellis Air Force Base). This event, which later became the equivalent of the Navy's "Top Gun" competition, included events of air-to-air gunnery "at altitudes of 10,000 and 20,000 feet, rocket firing, strafing, dive-bombing and skip-bombing."[85] Stewart was part of a three-man team that represented the 332nd Fighter Group and, as a result of their performance, won first place in the conventional fighter class.

"Oh, we got along really well and [Stewart] was one of the best pilots we had," Shipley said. "I can remember a couple of times he came back from a strafing run[86] and there was a bunch of gravel in the scoop under the plane. I guess he had gotten so close to the ground that the propeller sucked in the gravel and threw it back into the scoop [coolant air intake]—that's my only guess."

Grinning, he added, "After a couple of times of having to crawl under the plane and dig all of that gravel out by hand, I gave

---

[85] Gathering of Eagles, *Lieutenant Colonel Harry Stewart*, www.goefoundation.org.
[86] Strafing runs are the attack of ground targets made by an aircraft operating at a low altitude.

him a little bit of a hard time by telling him that he needed to try and get a little more altitude when he was out on those strafing runs."

When Stewart was asked about this situation, he mirthfully replied: "I guess I had flown in on a target pretty low!"

***

On December 29, 1944, the 332nd Fighter Group received an unexpected opportunity to serve as hosts to a group of white bomber pilots in dire need of assistance while on a mission. On this date, bad weather required that eighteen B-24 Liberators (seventeen from the 485th Bombardment Group and one from the 455th Bombardment Group) to make an emergency landing at Ramitelli when returning from a mission during which they had bombed an enemy railroad facility northern Italy. For the next five days, the white crews were provided with the best of hospitality that could be offered by the men of the 332nd Fighter Group.

"I remember them coming in," said Shipley of the arrival of the large bombers on the short airstrip accustomed to the smaller fighter planes. "We were all told to make room for the men so that they could spend the night in our tents, although none of the crew ended up staying in our tent," he added.

But not every member of 485th was appreciative of the hospitality that was extended to them by the men stationed at Ramitelli.

"I remember hearing about this one guy who said that he wasn't very happy about having to live in a tent with a bunch of black airmen, if even only for a few days," said Shipley. "The rest of the white crewmembers said they didn't care what he thought, they were going to stay with us," Shipley laughed. "I think he spouted off that he didn't know what his grandma would say [if he stayed with blacks] and he wasn't going to eat with us or sleep in the same tent as us." With a smile, he added, "I think that he ended up doing both."

In a letter dated January 6, 1945, Colonel Jack P. Tomhave of the 485th Bombardment Group sent a letter of appreciation to

Major E. Jones, Jr. of the 366th Air Squadron (a support element of the 332 Fighter Group) confirming his appreciation for the "courtesy and assistance" that was "so splendidly offered" to his crews [See *Appendix A*].

The ensuing days and weeks remained busy and passed by quickly, Shipley noted, and he and the men of the 332nd received not only the opportunity to participate in boxing matches, card games, choral and theater presentations on Ramitelli, but also enjoyed the excitement associated with the visits of several notable individuals.

"Yes, there were a bunch of different actors and famous people that came to see us at the base," Shipley affectionately recalled. "[Boxing champion] Joe Louis walked around the flight line talking to the guys and shaking hands."

Born Joseph Louis Barrow on May 13, 1914, near Lafayette, Alabama, Louis' obituary notes that he made his first appearance as a professional fighter on July 4, 1934. During World War II, he served in the Army and "traveled more than 21,000 miles and staged 96 boxing exhibitions before two million soldiers." He returned to professional boxing after leaving the service and went on to defend his boxing title twenty-five times, holding "the heavyweight boxing championship of the world for almost 12 years and the affection of the American public for most of his adult life..." wrote Deane McGowen in the April 13, 1981 edition of the *The New York Times*. Louis died at sixty-six years of age in Las Vegas, Nevada on April 12, 1981.

Also," Shipley continued, "Lena Horne came down the line and I got to meet and visit with her for a few seconds. Then she put on a show for us, too."

Lena Horne was born June 30, 1917 in Brooklyn, New York and "first achieved fame in the 1940s, becoming a nightclub and recording star in the 1950s and made a triumphant return to the spotlight with a one-woman Broadway show in 1981," as noted by Aljean Harmetz in the May 10, 2010 edition of *The New York Times*. Additionally, Harmetz's article notes that Horne toured several Army camps for the U.S.O. during World War II and that she "was outspoken in her criticism of the way black soldiers were treated."

Horne passed away on May 9, 2010 in Manhattan, New York at the age of ninety-two.

In addition to these celebrity visits, the crews were also rotated through periods of leave and granted several opportunities to leave the base to indulge themselves in the rich history and surreal splendor of the beautiful Italian countryside.

On a monthly basis, Shipley recalled, the men of the squadron would stand in a "pay line" to receive their wages. For Shipley, a portion of his pay went home to his parents, who would then put it in the bank for him; however, he still had enough money on his person to spend while on leave from his routine duties on the flight line.

"We all got some leave while we were at Ramitelli and I was able to travel to places like Naples, Sicily and Rome," Shipley said. "One of my buddies from St. Louis, Charlie Haynes, was assigned to my tent and we also did a lot of traveling together in our time off. In Rome, we got to see the catacombs and many of the old churches. In Italy," he elatedly stated, "I got the chance to ride a gondola (a traditional Italian flat-bottomed rowing boat), which was really a neat experience for a boy from Tipton! I remember looking down and seeing coins lying in the water in the bottom of the canals—that was really interesting."

Another fascinating irony of their visits throughout Italy, Shipley said, was that unlike much of the United States where Jim Crow prevented black citizens from being served at certain restaurants or denied entry into certain businesses, racism was not a prevalent concern when interacting with the Italian people.

In the book *Fighting in the Jim Crow Army*, author Maggi Morehouse describes the racist propaganda that often preceded black soldiers who were traveling throughout Italy. In one circumstance, signs were posted on billboards throughout the city of Naples that "threatened Italian women with violent reprisals if they engaged in any type of association with black soldiers."[87] Fortunately, such harsh and shameful measures were sporadic, short-lived and failed to

---

[87] Morehouse, *Fighting in the Jim Crow Army*, 172-173.

have the desired effect by those engaging in the discriminatory activities.

"At first," he said, the Italians were a little concerned about us because many of the white soldiers had spread all kinds of bad rumors about the black soldiers. But after we were around them and they learned that all of the bad things they had been told weren't true, we really didn't have any problems. The Italians treated us great," he said. "We could go anywhere we wanted and eat in any of the restaurants over there, too," he added.

Writing letters home was also a serious endeavor for many of the troops serving during the war—and the primary means of communication with family and loved ones—but was not an activity that Shipley viewed as a priority until the American Red Cross helped to change his perspective.

"I was never a very good at writing because when I was a young boy in school, one of my teachers made me change from writing with my left hand to writing with my right," he said. "So, I never wrote too many letters home until my mother contacted the Red Cross because she hadn't heard from me in awhile and didn't have any idea what was going on with me. As soon as the Red Cross representative got done talking to her, they got hold of me and gave me a chewing out and told me to write home," he chuckled, when recalling the incident.

As the days and weeks passed, Shipley remained at Ramitelli working under a hectic schedule to keep both his pilot and aircraft flying, until early May 1945, at which point the 332nd Fighter Group moved to Cattolica, Italy.[88] Shortly thereafter, the Germans surrendered and the group eventually made their final move to Lucera, Italy,[89] thus heralding the winding down of operations for the Tuskegee Airmen as their thoughts and reflections began to focus on the approaching movement back to the states.

---

[88] Cattolica is a town located along Italy's Adriatic coast and now become a major tourist destination in the region. It was home to nearby Cattolica Airfield during World War II, which has been abandoned since the war and was used by the 332nd Fighter Group for a period of only a few weeks.
[89] Lucera is a city located in the Foggia Province of Italy. As with Cattolica, it was home to a small airfield during World War II, which was also abandoned following the end of the war.

Chapter 6
Setting Sites on Home

"Never underestimate the power of dreams and the influence of the human spirit. We are all the same in this notion: The potential for greatness lives within each of us." - Wilma Rudolph

"Everybody seemed to be happy, to be honest with you," recalled Shipley when discussing the surrender of the German forces on May 8, 1945. "We had a little club that we all went to that night and let me tell you—it was packed!" he excitedly explained. "Truthfully, that was the only time in my life that I drank that much," he laughed.

Toward the end of the evening of their celebration in honor of the end of the war in Europe, a friend of Shipley's escorted him back to his tent, removed Shipley's pocketbook for safekeeping and then placed him in a cot to sleep off the spirits that had been consumed.

"When I woke up the next morning I had a bad headache and didn't know where I was at first," he said, mirthfully recalling the incident. "Then I noticed that my pocketbook was gone and I was really worried –it had all of my money in it and we had just gotten paid. But I soon found out that my friend had taken it off of me to make sure that nothing happened to it." He firmly concluded of the incident, "I have never drank like that since."

With the war now officially ended, many of the airmen would begin to cycle back to the United States; yet Shipley would remain overseas for nearly five more months before acquiring enough points to qualify for a discharge. The point system mentioned by Shipley was established toward the latter part of World War II "to release several million American soldiers from active service in Europe, though millions more had to be retained in order to continue the war against Japan."[90] To accomplish this monumental undertaking, the Army eventually developed a system that allowed soldiers who acquired eighty-five points or more to demobilize first. The criteria for accruing points were one point for every month in the Army; one point for every month served overseas; five points per campaign star or combat decoration (e.g., five points for each Purple Heart medal awarded); and, twelve points for each child a soldier had under eighteen, with up to three children credited.

For Shipley and the scores of men left behind due their lacking a sufficient number of points to warrant a discharge, their remaining days would often be spent with little work available to help pass their final days in Italy.

"After the war ended, most of us did the least amount of work that we could get away with," he smirked. "Things had been so busy with the war going on that it was nice to finally have a little down time so that we could finally relax a little. They had asked for a bunch of volunteers to go and work on vehicles and equipment in the motor pool but I knew not to volunteer for that … you should never volunteer for anything in the military because it usually doesn't end well for you when you do so," said Shipley, recalling a harsh lesson he had learned while still in training in the United States.

The aircraft that had in previous months become like members of the family to many of the pilots and crew chiefs soon disappeared from the Italian airfields, with little information given— other than rumors—regarding their final disposition. However, records indicate that the task of disposing of surplus aircraft no

---

[90] Young, *Equity in Theory and Practice*, 23.

longer needed for air battles was a task assigned to the "War Assets Administration, which later became the Reconstruction Finance Corp." In the carrying their responsibilities, this organization followed "regulations [that] set forth the costs and the procedures that enabled surplus war materiel to be transferred to schools and civic groups at minimal expense." [91]Planes, such as the P-51s utilized by the 332nd, were often times purchased for use as a memorial or educational resource by one of these organizations; however, the government retained ownership of the equipment and once no longer needed or desired by the municipality of civic group, the government required that the aircraft then be sold for scrap. Other times, the aircraft received no second life and was dismantled and sold for scrap and soon as it was determined it was longer required for further service.

Shipley noted, "When the war came to its end, we really no longer had any reason to hang on to the planes because we didn't have any missions to fly. I'm not really sure what happened to all of them because I didn't mess with them anymore and they kind of just disappeared one day. However," he soberly added, "there was one of the pilots that told us that they cut them up and scrapped them all. That would have made us crew chiefs just break down and cry to see something like that happen to our planes."

The waning weeks of their time in Italy also provided several opportunities for the men of the 332nd to visit a nearby towns, stroll down the streets and enjoy not only the company of the native people, but to consume the local faire as well. During these occasional outings, they discovered a small restaurant that served fish caught fresh daily, which soon became a favorite location among the soldiers and airmen.

When it came time for the balance of the 332nd to return to the United States in early October 1945, Shipley maintains, "They wanted some of us to volunteer to stay in [the military]," adding, "but I told them that I volunteered to join in the first place and that now it was time for me to get out and get on back home. Also,

---

[91] Veronico, *Hidden Warbirds II*, 180.

remember what I said about volunteering and how that usually plays out."

Once he and the 332nd arrived by troopship at Camp Kilmer, New Jersey on October 17, 1945, they began to disembark the ship, at which time, Shipley earnestly recalled, they received the following instructions by a white soldier on the pier responsible for guiding the returning troops to next in step in processing out of the military: "White soldiers to the right, niggers to the left," the unknown soldier bellowed.

Shipley somberly explained, "You can imagine how that made us feel … especially after how hard we worked and all of our accomplishments during the war. It really upset a lot us and we thought about grabbing at him. Some of the guys started mouthing back at the guy and it might have scared him enough that he changed his tune later down the line."

For the next couple of days, Shipley remained in New Jersey and was "asked a bunch of questions about the kind of schools I attended when I was in the service and what I did while I was over Italy," in addition to receiving his out-processing physical. He was then cleared to depart the post on October 19th and embarked on the next leg of his journey home. (The same day he left Camp Kilmer, the 301st Fighter Squadron was inactivated.)[92]

Soon, Shipley was aboard a train and on his way to Jefferson Barracks, Missouri,[93] where he was officially processed out of the Army and received his discharge papers on October 23, 1945 after accruing two years, eleven months and seventeen days of military service. While at the Army post, he was also given his mustering out and travel pay, and provided with a bus ticket for the trip back home.

---

[92] The 301st Fighter Squadron was inactivated on October 19, 1945, activated again on July 1, 1947, and inactivated on July 1, 1949.

[93] Established in 1826 as a permanent military reservation to replace Fort Bellefontaine, Jefferson Barracks served as an induction and separation center, a basic training site and the largest technical training school for the Army Air Corps during World War II. In 1946, the site was considered "excess" and has since that time become home to several National Guard and Reserve units. Jefferson Barracks Community Council, *History of Jefferson Barracks*, http://jbccstl.org.

Before leaving St. Louis, he stayed the night at the home of Charley Haynes[94]—the fellow aircraft mechanic who resided in his tent while the two were stationed in Ramitelli—where he was graciously treated to a long-awaited, delicious meal.

"That was quite a welcome back to the states," he said, remembering the details of the meal from decades past. "Charley was married and lived in St. Louis with his wife. When we got to his place, his wife put on quite some spread for us. I can remember there was a big roast, chicken, some mashed potatoes—you name it and she had it all laid out for us that day."

The next morning, he said his goodbyes and left his friend's home to board the bus that would carry him home to Tipton. Upon his arrival, the combat-experienced Shipley trekked the short distance across town to his parents' house and was extended a welcome similar to that which he had received when arriving in St. Louis.

"Mom had another big meal and I ended up stuffing myself with all kinds of good food again," he remarked. "That was something I could have easily gotten used to," he grinned.

---

[94] Charley Kemper Haynes was born June 14, 1910 and, according to records accessed through the National Archives, enlisted in the U.S. Army at Jefferson Barrack, Missouri on August 12, 1942. His occupation was listed as "Semiskilled Chauffeurs and Drivers, Bus, Taxi, Truck, and Tractor" and he went on to become a mechanic and attain the rank of technical sergeant in the U.S. Army Air Forces while serving alongside Shipley in the 301st Fighter Squadron. Following the war, Haynes went on to retire from the United States Postal Service, died on April 3, 1995 and is buried in the Jefferson Barracks National Cemetery.

When Shipley returned home in 1945, his younger brother David was away from home, serving in the U.S. Navy. He was discharged in 1946 after serving as a coxswain at the Naval Air Station in Pensacola, Florida. **Courtesy of the Dr. David O. Shipley, Sr. family**

The reunion back home was grand and memorable, Shipley said, although it would be awhile before he would again see his younger brother David O. Shipley, who had been drafted into the United States Navy on September 10, 1943 and served as a coxswain at the Navy Air Station at Pensacola, Florida, until receiving his honorable discharge on May 25, 1946. David O. Shipley, Sr. was born in Tipton, Missouri on June 9, 1925. Following his service during World War II, he became an ordained as a minister and received his Bachelor of Divinity degree, Master of Divinity degree, and a Doctorate of Ministry in Marriage and Family Counseling. The younger Shipley was the author of several books and became the first black chaplain of the Kansas City, Missouri, Police Department and was pastor of churches in Arkansas, Kansas, Texas and Missouri in both the Presbyterian and Baptist denominations. In addition to penning several articles for the Kansas City Star, Shipley was selected as one of the 100 Most Influential Preachers by the Kansas City Globe and received an Image Award from the Urban League of Greater Kansas City, Missouri. He married Alberta D. Scott in 1952 and, following her death in 1976, married Earma Jean Rencher the following year. The father of four sons, David Shipley, Sr. passed away on March 11, 2002 and is interred in Mt. Moriah Cemetery in Kansas City, Missouri.

Shipley's older brother, Lee Frederick Shipley, was living in the Kansas City area and employed as a magnetic inspector at the North American Aviation Plant when his younger brother made his return from the war. Lee Frederick Shipley was born in Tipton on April 26, 1914 and later moved to Kansas to attend Western Baptist College. The elder Shipley followed in the educational footsteps of his father by also attending Lincoln University in Jefferson City, and completed extension work from the University of Missouri and the University of Kansas. Married to Etha Delois Thomas in 1938, he was the father of four children. According to his obituary, in addition to his many employment pursuits, he also owned the Shipley Realty Company and was a realtor for more than fifty years. Lee Shipley passed away on August 12, 2005 and is interred in Park Lawn Cemetery-Memorial Park in Kansas City, Missouri.

Shipley's younger sister, Rosalind, was still living at home at the time of her brother's return. As James Shipley noted, his younger sister was born in 1928 and later married a gentleman from nearby California, Missouri, and became Rosalind Russell. She worked for many years as a secretary for a school system in Kansas City while her husband was employed as a school teacher. She still resides in Kansas City as of the publication of this book.

The late Leland Ronald Shipley, right, was approximately three months old when adopted by James Shipley's parents in November 1945. He followed in the footsteps of his brothers by serving in the military, spending more than twenty-one years in the United States Navy. Courtesy of the Dr. David O. Shipley, Sr. family

Approximately two weeks after reuniting with the family from whom he had been separated during his lengthy overseas deployment, Shipley said, his parents adopted a young boy, adding the sixth and final child to the Shipley family. Leland Ronald Shipley was born August 14, 1945 and would have been approximately three months old when adopted by Galveston and Frances Shipley. He joined the Navy after attending schools in Tipton (retiring after more than 20 years of military service) and married Mildred Marie Dickey Walker on October 18, 1981, a union to which three children were born. He passed away on April 27, 2008 and is buried in the Fort Sill National Cemetery in Oklahoma.

"I remember when they brought home our adopted brother, Leland, he was so tiny that they carried him in a Pepsi Cola box," he said.

The time had come for Shipley to begin the process of returning to life as a civilian, while never clinging to the belief that his experiences with the 332nd Fighter Group would soon develop into a revered piece of the American military legend of World War II. Also, the veteran added, his return from reputable overseas combat service did not seem to find him very far removed from the contemptible and oftentimes lingering presence of racism.

After the war, Shipley said, he decided to pay a visit to his older sister, Miriam "Geraldine" McCreary, who was born in Tipton on March 28, 1921, the first daughter and second child of Galveston and Frances Shipley. After attending grade school and high school in Tipton and graduating as valedictorian of her class, she went to attend Western College and Lincoln University. She was married in 1939 and lived a life epitomizing the voluntary spirit, spending many years as a devoted member of Second Baptist Church in Kansas City, Missouri, and also serving as a Den Mother for The Boy Scouts of America, a member of Jack and Jill of America and actively involved in her children's' school PTAs. She passed away on May 23, 2000 and is buried in Mt. Moriah Cemetery in Kansas City.

"When I got to Kansas City to visit Geraldine, I was wearing my uniform and decided I would first stop by this place that sells ice cream. I went to the drive-up window and the lady working there told me that she was not allowed to serve me; she said that I would have to go around back to be served since I was black."

With a somber pause, he concluded, "As I said, I had on my uniform and everything and I thought that might mean something. We believed that our performance in the war had helped break up the segregation in the service—which it did, later—but it was hard to believe that this type of thing was still happening when we came back home. It was one of those situations that was really hard to understand and very upsetting."

Thus began the Tuskegee Airman's bewildering introduction to post-war America.

Chapter 7
Family, God and New Horizons

"I believe that the United States as a government, if it is going to be true to its own founding documents, does have the job of working toward that time when there is no discrimination made on such inconsequential reason as race, color, or religion." . –Pres. Dwight D. Eisenhower

At his home in Tipton, Shipley takes a few moments to sift through pages of old military photographs while reflecting upon his time as a mechanic with the Tuskegee Airmen.

When he returned to his hometown, the former airman made the decision to live with his parents for awhile and devote himself to working as a mechanic, thus allowing him the opportunity to begin saving money for his future. His father, Galveston, was pleased to see his son, who had spent more than eleven months overseas, return safely from the dangers of living and working in a combat zone.

Douglas Shipley, youngest son of Dr. David O. Shipley, Sr. (and nephew to Jim Shipley) noted in a 2016 interview that Galveston was known to commemorate special events in his family's life through the writing of poetry. One such poem highlighted the pride he possessed in the military service of his sons (that of both James and younger brother David) in addition to showing the satisfaction he maintained for the postwar career paths they chose to pursue and the faith they demonstrated in their adult lives.

The Bible Boys

We read our Bible and loved it
And admired many of its great men.
So as boys in our family tree flit,
David and James were names chosen then.
Not twins but they stood shoulder to shoulder
In stature as they went on their way,
James the older was somewhat bolder;
Yet, David dreamed the dreams each day,
That kept the two in constant view
Of others who searched for the new.

After finishing the little school in town,
War came and they were found.
James, in the air corps busy;
David, on the gulf waters dizzy.
As the war dragged on in years,
And parents shed so many tears,
Both came back well and strong,
And today they travel along
James, a mechanic, doctoring engines' ills;
David, a preacher, swaying human wills.

--Galveston Shipley

A number of years would pass before the former fighter plane mechanic would fully realize the magnitude of the contributions made by the dedicated and hardworking men of the 332nd Fighter Group. But it was less than two years following Shipley's discharge from the U.S. Army Air Forces that there arrived an integral moment in the quest for civil rights; an event that was ushered into society by a fellow Missourian—President Harry S. Truman. Issued on July 26, 1948, Executive Order 9981 became the mandate through which President Truman officially desegregated the U.S. military and was "met with so much opposition from some of the armed services, especially the army, that its requirements were not completely fulfilled until 1954."[95] Additionally, reflection on this cardinal component of the civil rights agenda of the Truman administration has been viewed by some historians as not only a means through which the president could correct past wrongs, but also "a way for Truman to get control of his party and stay ahead of rapidly changing political attitudes" during what was perceived as a "hotly contested upcoming election." [96]

Whether for political expediency or based upon an earnest desire to provide equality for those who had sacrificed greatly for the very country that had for so long denied them equality, many of the black airmen returning from Italy simply wanted to get on with their lives, find work and possibly build a strong home and family, leaving behind the hardships of overseas service.

For the first three years following his discharge, Shipley returned to the employment position he had held prior to the war: working for his friend, Paul Miller, at his automotive garage and Studebaker dealership in Tipton. In search of a higher paycheck, he then found a position at a Cadillac and Pontiac Dealership several miles away in Boonville, where he began applying his skills in their shop as a mechanic.

"I think I did that for two or three years until I finally got tired of driving back and forth every day," he said. "There was one night when it was really foggy," he explained, "and I was returning home from work. I almost ran up into the back end of a big truck –I couldn't see him!

---

[95] Mershon &Schlossman, *Foxholes& Color Lines*, xi.
[96] Morehouse, *Fighting in the Jim Crow Army*, 211.

That's when I decided it was time for me to find something a little closer to home."

Shipley, far left, is pictured in the early 1950s while working as a mechanic for the Chevrolet dealership in Tipton. He would leave this job to open his own garage in town, which he operated for nearly four years. Courtesy of Jim Shipley

Back in Tipton, changes and new beginnings continued to arrive as Shipley found employment as a mechanic at the local Chevrolet dealership; however, it was his decision to accompany his father to a local track meet that would bring about one of the most profound changes in his life and lay the foundation for a new relationship that would in later years lead to the establishment of a family of his own.

"Harrison School was participating in a track meet against a bunch of other local schools—in 1946, I believe—over in New Franklin [Missouri]," said Shipley. "I took my dad over there and that's when I saw her for the first time," he sheepishly grinned."

While at the event, Shipley spied Mildred Bruce, a Boonville native who was dressed in her cheerleading outfit to help root for her school during the track meet. Eventually mustering the courage to make an approach, the Red Tails veteran sauntered over to speak with the attractive woman, who had effortlessly managed to capture his interest.

"She gave me her telephone number and we began dating not long after that," Shipley said. "I would go over to pick her up at her parents' house and then we would go to a restaurant or some little place to spend some time together. We went to some dances in the area, I remember, because she loved to dance ... but I never did like dancing because I couldn't do much more than step all over her feet," he boisterously laughed.

Since he was a few years older than Mildred, Shipley believed that he would somehow need to prove himself to her parents to gain their approval and demonstrate his commitment to their daughter. With his background as a mechanic, it was not long before he was able to identify a means by which to ingratiate himself with her father.

"Well, her father had this old Chevrolet car that got to the point where it finally needed a new engine," he explained. "He was going to buy an engine from Sears and Roebuck but since I was working at the Chevrolet dealership, I told him that I could save him some money and get him an engine at a discount from the garage, which I did," he added. "When I finally got the engine, I went over to their house one Sunday afternoon and put it in for him—even though I never really liked working on Sundays," Shipley affirmed. "After that, we both got along just fine.

Next, Shipley embarked upon his quest to find a way to curry favor with the mother of his new girlfriend.

"Millie [Mildred] told me that her mom really liked ice cream, so I began taking a quart of ice cream over there just about every time I would come to their house for a visit. We soon got along just fine, too," he wryly noted.

Following three years of courtship, the couple traveled to Kansas City and married on December 7, 1949.

James Shipley is pictured with his wife, Mildred, in this family photograph taken in the late 1980s. Standing, from left, is their children: Kenneth (oldest), Cynthia McPherson (second oldest) and Timothy (youngest). Courtesy of James and Mildred Shipley.

He continued working at the Chevrolet dealership in Tipton until a "falling out" with his boss encouraged him to pursue a different direction in his career. One day, Shipley noted, he left work to stop by the local shoe store to purchase a new pair of work boots. During his brief absence, a woman from the community stopped by the garage requesting that Shipley perform some maintenance work on her vehicle.

"My boss was angry that I wasn't there when the lady stopped by looking for me," he said. "He told me that I had a family to support and that I'd better straighten up if I wanted to keep my job. We had never really gotten along very well and I had reached the point where I had finally had enough; I knew it was time to find something else."

Shipley soon chose to embrace the offer extended by another local mechanic who ran a garage in town but was ready to sell out of the business. Approaching a local banker to acquire the finances necessary to purchase the garage, Shipley was turned down for a loan and warned that "he'd better stay [at the Chevrolet dealership]" because that was the "best [he] could do for himself." In a fortuitous twist, the building in which the garage was housed was the property of George Safire—his old friend for whom he had shined shoes as a young boy—and Shipley was able to borrow the money from him to purchase the business.

"George always liked me and trusted me enough give me the money that I needed to purchase the business," Shipley said. "I worked hard and was able to pay off the loan within a year," he added.

The early 1950s remained a busy time for Shipley as he continued to repair the vehicles of local residents, although this time the work was done as a self-employed mechanic.

"I worked for myself until one day I left the garage to go pick something up and my [oldest] son Kenneth, who was really just a baby at the time, was chasing my car … running down the middle of the highway. He could have been hit and killed," he added. "That shook me up enough that I decided it was time to find something else to do."

A local company, Co-Mo Electric Cooperative, Inc.,[97] began bringing some of their vehicles to Shipley's garage for assorted types of repairs. When he learned that the company was taking their vehicles to other shops as well, he made them a promise that would lead to his next and final job as a professional mechanic.

---

[97] The website for the Co-Mo Electric Cooperative, Inc., explains that the energy cooperative found its roots in the Rural Electrification Administration—a government entity created during the Great Depression that provided "low interest loans to investor owned utilities to encourage them to stretch out their lines from middle America's cities into the countryside. Co-Mo received its name from the first two letters of each of the four original counties in the cooperative, which was Cooper, Cole, Moniteau and Morgan. The cooperative energized its first section of line on December 24, 1939, has headquarters in Tipton and around eighty employees. Co-Mo Electric Cooperative, Inc., *Co-Mo History*, www.co-mo.coop/.

Hiring on with the company in 1956, Shipley noted that he "guaranteed them that if I didn't show them within six months' time that I was able to save them money on their vehicle maintenance and repairs, that they wouldn't have to ask me to leave—I'd leave on my own," he avowed. "I spent twenty-nine years [with Co-Mo], working on engines, putting in windshields, doing transmission work—the whole nine yards." He continued, "About the only thing that I didn't do while I was working for them was change the tires on their big trucks."

As the years passed by quickly, the Shipley's welcomed the addition of their second child, Cynthia, followed by another son (and final child) Timothy. Moving into a house situated next door to the building that formerly housed the Harrison School (where Shipley's father had taught for many years), the veteran has maintained both his Christian faith and membership at the Prairie Grove Baptist Church, where he was served as a deacon for several decades.

Shipley and his wife have donated countless hours to their community during the seventeen years they operated a summer camp near Knob Knoster, Missouri. Not only did he and his wife assist with the cooking and cleaning, but they also helped coordinate events such as Bible lessons, baseball games and arts and crafts to keep the children engaged and entertained.

"It was really a camp for black children," Shipley stated. "Back in the 1950s, society hadn't really reached the point where black kids could attend camps with white children, so we wanted to make sure that they would have a place to learn and socialize with other black children."

Years later, when church camps in the areas were finally desegregated, the Shipleys would use their personal vacation time every summer to prepare meals at a camp at Lake of the Ozarks in central Missouri for a local Baptist association.

During a ceremony held on September 8, 2007 at the Truman Presidential Library and Museum in Independence, Missouri, Shipley received replica Congressional Gold Medal in honor of the accomplishments of the Tuskegee Airmen during World War II. Shipley is pictured with his wife, Mildred. Courtesy of James Shipley

Regardless of the many voluntary endeavors he and Millie pursued, remaining positively engaged in the lives of the children of the community, Shipley's thoughts have never deviated very far from his military service and he has chosen to remain involved in events intended to recognize the contributions he and his fellow airmen made during the Second World War and beyond.

"Sometime … oh, back several years ago, some of the former 332nd guys started receiving an invitation to attend the big air show that is held over in Columbia [Missouri].[98] All of the Tuskegee

[98] *The Salute to Veterans Celebration and Air Show* was founded in 1989 "[t]o recognize, honor and thank all veterans of the Armed Services of the United States of America, past and present, who have served their country, both living and dead," as noted on the organization's website. Held on Memorial Day weekend,

Airmen would stay in the same hotel, meet up for awhile to kind of visit amongst ourselves, eat a little dinner and then go down to the flight line and enjoy all of the sites and activities," he said. "It was really about a weeklong event and while we were there, some of the guys were scheduled to go to speak at some of the local schools or for different community organizations." He added, "They still do the air show every year and have even had P-51 Mustangs and other World War II planes on display that we used to work on and fly, which really does bring back a lot of memories for all of us."

Another exciting and unexpected opportunity arrived for Shipley in 2007; when President George W. Bush presented the Tuskegee Airmen with the Congressional Gold Medal in recognition of their stellar record in combat—a history that includes "15,000 combat sorties flown, 260 enemy aircraft destroyed, 1,000 black pilots flew missions, 150 Flying Crosses and Legions of Merit earned, and more than 700 Air Medals and clusters earned"[99]—all of which was made possible by Shipley and the scores of ground crews that kept the planes running as efficiently as possible and often receiving little credit for having done such [See Appendix B]. Although Shipley was not part of the entourage who attended the official ceremony in Washington, D.C., ceremonies were held in other locations nationwide to ensure that bronze replicas of the original gold medal were presented to the remaining members of the 332nd Fighter Group.

On September 8, 2007, many former Tuskegee Airmen, including Shipley, made the trip to the Truman Presidential Library and Museum in Independence, Missouri. During a ceremony attended by members of Congress and several local dignitaries, Shipley and several fellow 332nd veterans each received their replica of the Congressional Gold Medal—more than sixty years after they had left the service [See Appendix C].

---

the organization now has three hundred volunteers and one hundred committee chairmen. Posner, *Our History*, www.salute.org.
[99] The Official Homepage of the U.S. Army, *President, Congress Honor Tuskegee Airmen*, www.army.mil.

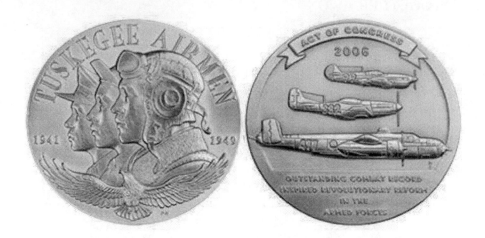

Pictured is the Congressional Gold Medal presented to the Tuskegee Airmen collectively as a group. Many individual members of the Tuskegee Airmen received bronze replicas of the medal during special ceremonies held throughout the country. The front of the medal features the profiles of three airmen: the first is a pilot wearing a leather flying helmet; the second a ground mechanic; and the third is a pilot wearing a service hat. Also depicted is a soaring eagle below the three profiles. The reverse side of the medal features the profiles of three aircraft, which are from top to bottom: a Curtiss P-40 with "99" on the fuselage; a P-51D Mustang with "332" on fuselage; and a B-25 with "477" on the fuselage. The numbers on the fuselage represent the flight groups of black aviators who served during the war. **Public domain**

"It was a very interesting ceremony," said Shipley when describing the event. "The Kansas City mayor made a big talk and they had a flyover with a couple of planes. Two guys parachuted out of the planes and landed in an area right down below where we were seated." He excitedly added," Those guys were wearing backpacks that they used to carry the medals that they ended up giving to us in the ceremony."

James Shipley, left, is paused for a photograph alongside a fellow World War II veteran after they returned from a trip to Washington, D.C., as part of the Central Missouri Honor Flight—a program that takes certain veterans, free-of-charge, to see the war memorials at the nation's capital. Courtesy of James Shipley

With humility, he added, "I never thought in my lifetime that we would ever receive something like that because we had all just done our duty over in Italy. I'm pretty sure that none of us ever expected any type of recognition for it."

The excitement from pleasant reflection continued when the former airman described his opportunity to travel to Washington, D.C., as part of the tenth *Central Missouri Honor Flight* that took place in late August 2013. The *Central Missouri Honor Flight* is part of the Honor Flight Network, a non-profit organization that "transports our heroes from throughout Central Missouri to Washington, D.C., to visit and reflect at their memorials at no cost to them."[100]

---

[100] Central Missouri Honor Flight, *About Central Missouri Honor Flight,* http://centralmissourihonorflight.com.

The excitement from pleasant reflection continued when the former airman described his opportunity to travel to Washington, D.C., as part of the tenth *Central Missouri Honor Flight* that took place in late August 2013. The *Central Missouri Honor Flight* is part of the Honor Flight Network, a non-profit organization that "transports our heroes from throughout Central Missouri to Washington, D.C., to visit and reflect at their memorials at no cost to them."[101] Although priority has been given to World War II veterans, Korean War and Vietnam era veterans are also eligible for trip to see the war memorials in the nation's capitol, all of which is completed in one day and does not require an overnight stay.

Many veterans who completed the Honor Flight trip ecstatically recall the reception they received upon their return. "Children, up hours past their bedtimes, waved flags, and elderly family members stood up from wheelchairs to clap and cheer," wrote Christie Megura in an article that was printed in the August 26, 2013 edition of the *Columbia Missourian* newspaper. "In a sea of stars and stripes, the excitement was contagious," she added.[102]

"Again," Shipley said, "it was one of those times that I was really shocked by all of the appreciation we were shown ... especially for something that I had done so many decades earlier." With a soft grin, he concluded, "It was a touching situation to be able to see the World War II memorial and visit and share stories with many of my fellow veterans. It was all quite impressive and something that I will never forget."

---

[101] Central Missouri Honor Flight, *About Central Missouri Honor Flight,* http://centralmissourihonorflight.com.
[102] Megura, *Missouri veterans connect future, past through Honor Flight,* www.columbiamissourian.com.

James Shipley, left, shares a humorous moment with fellow World War II veteran Edward "Babe" Gross—who completed 72 combat missions in the South Pacific as a radio operator aboard a B-25 Mitchell—inside the office of Missouri Gov. Jay Nixon prior to receiving the Silver Star Banner during a ceremony on April 30, 2014. Courtesy of Shawn C. Johnson

The accolades continued to arrive, this time on April 30, 2014, when Missouri Governor Jay Nixon remarked, "During each of our country's wars, Missourians have stepped forward to serve, and have done so with courage and self-sacrifice. These four veterans are among the many who incurred injury or illness while in harm's way, and I am pleased to help honor their service to our state and nation with this award. As we observe Silver Star Families of America Day on May 1, we are reminded of the sacrifices that our military veterans have made, and continue to make, on our behalf."[103]

In 2016, Shipley and his wife received an invitation to attend special ceremonies that were held in Tuskegee, Alabama,

---

[103] Office of Missouri Governor Jay Nixon, *Gov. Nixon presents four Missouri veterans*, https://governor.mo.gov.

commemorating the seventy-fifth anniversary of the activation of the U.S. Army Air Corps' 99th Pursuit Squadron at Chanute Field on March 22, 1941, which is now recognized as the official birth date of the Tuskegee Airmen. This event, Shipley sagely noted, served as a demonstration of the great strides that have been made in race relations since the end of the Second World War.

"The first time I was at Tuskegee, back in the '40s, you could hardly walk down the sidewalk without being harassed or called some kind of despicable name," he recalled. "You really weren't allowed to go any place in town, either. But when we were down there recently for the anniversary celebration, you couldn't even tell that segregation had ever existed—everything had changed ... even attitudes!" he exclaimed. "Now you can go visit any restaurant that you want or go anywhere in town and not have to worry about being harassed because of the color of your skin."

The recent years have also found the veteran busily engaged in managing and maintaining rental houses around the community of Tipton and "trying to keep [his] grass cut," he laughingly shared. Now several decades removed from the hardships of a dusty airstrip in Ramitelli, Italy, Shipley has taken the time to reflect on the profound moments of which he has been witness, and has come to understand the legacy that he and his fellow Red Tails will leave behind for not only those black men and women who choose to take up the mantle of military service, but African Americans in all walks of life.

The record of the 332nd Fighter Group has reached near legendary status since the end of the World War II and garnered much notoriety for many who served within the ranks of the distinguished organization. "By March 1945, the 332nd had flown more than 200 missions including strafing attacks on ground targets and fighter sweeps as well as bomber escort missions." The group eventually added to this record by flying "179 bomber escort missions out of a total of 311 missions for the Fifteenth Air Force."[104] With such a record and list of accomplishments, it is of little surprise that lights of accolade have shined upon the many pilots who flew these missions and ceremonies have been held to honor the aviators who gave their lives overseas; but far from the

---

[104] Haulman, *The Tuskegee Airmen and the "Never Lost a Bomber Myth*, 2.

limelight has remained the brave men on the ground who turned the wrenches that kept the aircraft in peak operational condition.

Colonel (Ret.) Gerald D. Curry sagely noted that "[b]lacks have fought in every major military conflict in which America has ever engaged." He also emphasized that it is "imperative" for aspiring black military officers to "learn the stories of Buffalo Soldiers and Tuskegee Airmen" since the details of such service were not stressed during his high school or undergraduate training.[105] However, although 138,903 black enlisted members were serving in the Army Air Forces as of June 1945, which greatly outnumbered the 1,559 black officers serving during the same period,[106] most of the works that detail the contributions of the Tuskegee Airmen often center on the contributions of the officers and pilots and not the performance of the ground crews; yet stories such as Shipley's can help ensure the legacy of these enlisted soldiers are never again relegated to the back pages of history.

Drawing upon years of experiences with a mindset forged in the cauldron of both hardships and blessings, Shipley said, "All these years later, it was kind of a surprise to me when the movie[107] came out and showed everybody just what we went through—I just never thought they would make a film about what we did or that anybody would be all that interested in all that we accomplished. I like to think that I did my part in all of this by making sure those planes were ready to go and could do their job when they took off from the air strip every day … and that we [on the ground crews] not only helped win the war, but that the planes we kept operational helped send many men back home that otherwise wouldn't have made it."

In humble contemplation and with hesitance to curry favor or credit for any role he may have played in the successful record of the 332nd Fighter Group, Shipley noted, "At first, they had set us up as an experiment … they said we'd never make the grade. There were those in the military who believed that we'd get scared in combat

---

[105] Curry, *Striving for Perfection*, 2.
[106] Osur, *Blacks in the Army Air Forces During World War II*, 137.
[107] Here Shipley is referring to the 2012 film "Red Tails."

and just take off and run scared. But I've always believed in the motto 'United we stand, divided we fall,' and if we hadn't eventually joined together as a country and learned to work together as one, we may not have been able to win the war."

Appendix A

Below is a copy of the letter that was sent by the on behalf of the 485th Bombardment Group expressing their appreciation for the hospitality they received after making an emergency landing at the air field in Ramitelli on December 29, 1944.

Headquarters
485th Bombardment Group (H)
APO 529   US ARMY

6 January 1945

Major E. Jones, Jr.
366th Air Service Squadron
APO 520, US Army

Dear Major Jones,

On behalf of the Officers and Enlisted Men of 485th Bombardment Group, I want to personally thank you for the courtesy and assistance which you and the personnel of the 366th Air Service Squadron so splendidly offered to our crews which landed at your base on 29 December 1944. I fully realize what an inconvenience this forced landing must have made on your facilities, and the remarkable manner in which you people of the 15th Fighter Command rose to the situation is all the more commendable.

The very able assistance which your Service Squadron has given to the 332nd Fighter Group is well known, and now you have proven yourselves just as capable in servicing our heavy bombers.

Sincerely Y yours,
/s/Jack P. Tomhave
JACK P. TOMHAVE
Colonel, Air Corps
Commanding

Appendix B

Below is a copy of the remarks made by President George W. Bush on March 29, 2007 at the U.S. Capitol during a Congressional Gold Medal Ceremony honoring members of the Tuskegee Airmen.

THE PRESIDENT: Thank you all. Please be seated. Thank you. Madam Speaker, Mr. Leader, members of Congress, Secretary Powell, distinguished guests: You know, the Speaker and I had the honor of having our picture taken with you, and as I walked into the rotunda, a place that occasionally I get invited up here and I walk into, I was impressed by the fact that I wasn't amongst heroes who were statues. I was impressed that I was amongst heroes who still live. (Applause.) I thank you for the honor you have brought to our country. And the medal you're about to receive means our country honors you, and rightly so.

I want to thank Senator Carl Levin and Sergeant Rangel. (Laughter.) Excuse me, Mr. Chairman. (Applause.) I thank you for your leadership on this issue. I have a strong interest in World War II airmen. I was raised by one. He flew with a group of brave young men who endured difficult times in the defense of our country. Yet for all they sacrificed and all they lost, in a way, they were very fortunate, because they never had the burden of having their every mission, their every success, their every failure viewed through the color of their skin. Nobody told them they were a credit to their race. Nobody refused to return their salutes. Nobody expected them to bear the daily humiliations while wearing the uniform of their country.

It was different for the men in this room. When America entered World War II, it might have been easy for them to do little for our country. After all, the country didn't do much for them. Even the Nazis asked why African American men would fight for a country that treated them so unfairly. Yet the Tuskegee airmen were eager to join up.

You know, I'm interested in the story about a young man who was so worried that the Army might change its mind about allowing him to fly, that he drove immediately to the train station. He left his car, as well as $1,000 worth of photography equipment. He never saw his car, he never saw his camera, but he became a flyer.

These men in our presence felt a special sense of urgency. They were fighting two wars: One was in Europe, and the other took place in the hearts and minds of our citizens. That's why we're here. The white commander of the Tuskegee airfield was once asked -- with all seriousness -- how do African Americans fly? -- reflecting the ignorance of the times, they said, how do African Americans fly? He said, "Oh, they fly just like everybody else flies -- stick and rudder." Soon, Americans in their kitchens and living rooms were reading the headlines. You probably didn't realize it at the time, but you were making headlines at home, headlines that spoke about daring pilots winning a common battle.

And little by little, every victory at war was translated to a victory here in the United States. And we're in the presence of men who are earning those victories, important victories, leaders who pierced the unquestioned prejudices of a different society. You gave African Americans a sense of pride and possibility.

You saw that pride and awe, I'm sure you remember, in the faces of young children who came up to you right after the war and tugged and your uniforms and said, "Mister, can you really fly an airplane?" Some of you have been in Germany and Iraq, and you still see that sense of pride.

I appreciate your going. I appreciate the fact that one of our young soldiers today took pictures for -- of you for a scrapbook for his children. I appreciate the fact that one of our soldiers today said, "It's not often that you get a chance to meet the guys who have paved the path for you." (Applause.)

The Tuskegee Airmen helped win a war, and you helped change our nation for the better. Yours is the story of the human spirit, and it ends like all great stories do -- with wisdom and lessons and hope for tomorrow. And the medal that we confer today means that we're doing a small part to ensure that your story will be told and honored for generations to come. (Applause.)

And I would like to offer a gesture to help atone for all the unreturned salutes and unforgivable indignities. And so, on behalf of the office I hold, and a country that honors you, I salute you for the service to the United States of America. (Applause.)

Appendix C

Below is a copy of the program that was given to attendees during the
Congressional Gold Medal Ceremony held at the Truman Presidential
Library in Independence, Missouri, on September 8, 2007.

PROGRAM

Prelude . . . . American Legion Band

Master of Ceremony . . . . .Col. (USAF-Ret.) T. Len Nevels

Presentation of Colors .Color Guards

National Anthem . . . . .American Legion Band

Invocation . . . . .Rev. Dr. Margaret N. Roberts

Pastor, Swope Parkway

United Christian Church

Salute to Tuskegee Airmen . . . . .Commemorative Air Force

Introduction of Dignitaries . . . . Col. T. Len Nevels

Welcome and Remarks . . . . . . .Honorable Emanual Cleaver II

U.S. Congressman

Missouri's Fifth District

Remarks on Resolution (HR 1259) . . . Honorable Dennis Moore

U.S. Congressman

Kansas' Third District

Introduction of Keynote Speaker . . . . .Col T. Len Nevels

Keynote Speaker . . . . Col. (USAF Ret.) Charles McGee

Tuskegee Airman

Delivery of Congressional Gold Medals . .Missouri River Sky Divers

Tuskegee Airmen Medal Presentation . . . . ,Congressmen

Cleaver and Moore

Posthumously
Honorees

Closing Remarks . . . . .President Edward King

Benediction . . . . .Chaplain Major Robert N. Phillips

Whiteman Air Base

Retire Colors . . . . .Col. T. Len Nevels

WORKS CITED

NEWSPAPERS

Columbia Missourian (Columbia, Missouri)
Daily Capital News (Jefferson City, Missouri)
The New York Times (New York, New York)
The Pittsburgh Press (Pittsburgh, Pennsylvania)

BOOKS AND ARTICLES

Booker, M. Keith (editor). *Comics Through Time: A History of Icons, Idols and Ideas*. (Santa Barbara, CA: ABC-CLIO, 2014).

Bracey, Earnest. Daniel *"Chappie" James: The First African American Four Star General*. (Jefferson, North Carolina: McFarland & Company, Inc., 2003).

Brady, Tim. *The American Aviation Experience: A History*. (Carbondale & Edwardsville, IL: Southern Illinois University Press, 2000.)

Bucholtz, Chris. *332nd Fighter Group—Tuskegee Airmen*. (Oxford, UK: Osprey Publishing, 2007).

Caver, Joseph, Ennels, Jerome & Daniel Haulman. *The Tuskegee Airmen: An Illustrated History, 1939-1949*. (Montgomery, AL: NewSouth Books, 2011).

Craven, Wesley F. & Cate, James L. *The Army Air Forces in World War II, Volume Six: Men and Planes*. (Washington, D.C.: U.S. Government Printing Office, 1983).

Curry, Col. (RET) Gerald D. *Striving for Perfection: Developing Professional Black Officers*. (Bloomington, IN: Curry Brothers Marketing and Publishing Group, 2013).

Fletcher, Larry E. *Moniteau County Schools History*. (Versailles, MO: B-W Graphics, Inc., 1984).

Francis, Charles E. *The Tuskegee Airmen: The Men Who Changed a Nation*. (Wellesley, MA: Branden Publishing Company, 2008).

Harris, Jaqueline. *The Tuskegee Airmen: Black Heroes of World War II*. (Parsippany, NJ: Dillon Press, 1996).

Haulman, Daniel. *The Tuskegee Airmen and the "Never Lost a Bomber Myth*. (Montgomery, AL: NewSouth Books, 2011).

Homan, Lynn & Thomas Reilly. *Black Knights: The Story of the Tuskegee Airmen*. (Gretna, LA: Pelican Publishing Company, Inc., 2001).

Tischauser, Leslie. *Jim Crow Laws*. (Santa Barbara, CA: ABC-CLIO, 2012).

Jakeman, Robert J. *The Divided Skies: Establishing Segregated Flight Training at Tuskegee, Alabama, 1934*-1942. (Tuscaloosa, AL: The University of Alabama Press, 1992).

Lee, Ulysses. *The Employment of Negro Troops*. (Washington, D.C.: Center of Military History, United States Army, 2001).

Manitelli-Brown-Kittel-Graf, *Bell P-39 Airacobra, Bell P-63 Kingcobra*. (Edizioni R.E.I., 2015).

Mershon, Sherie & Steven Schlossmann. *Foxholes & Color Lines: Desegregating the U.S. Armed Forces. (Baltimore, MD: The John Hopkins University Press, 1998)*.

Miller, Francis Trevelyan. *History of World War II*. (Philadelphia: The John C. Winston Company, 1945).

Molesworth, Carl. *Curtiss P-40: Long-nosed Tomahawks*. (Oxford, UK: Osprey Publishing, 2013).

Moniteau County Historical Society. *History of Moniteau County, Missouri, Volume II*. (Marceline, MO: Walsworth Publishing Company, Inc., 2000).

Moore, Arthur. *A Careless Word -- a Needless Sinking: A History of the Staggering Losses Suffered by the U.S. Merchant Marine, Both in Ships and Personnel, During World War II.* (United Maritime Service Veterans, 2001).

Morehouse, Maggie M. *Fighting in the Jim Crow Army: Black Men and Women Remember World War II.* (Lanham, MD: Rowman & Littlefield Publishers, Inc., 2000).

Moye, J. Todd. *Freedom Flyers: The Tuskegee Airmen of World War II.* (New York, NY: Oxford University Press, Inc., 2010).

Munson, Kenneth. *Fighters: 1939-1945.* (London, UK: Bounty Books, 2012).

Nolen, Rose M. *African Americans in Mid-Missouri: From Pioneers to Ragtimers.* (Charleston, SC: The History Press, 2010).

Osur, Alan M. *Blacks in the Army Air Forces During World War II.* (Washington, D.C.: U.S. Government Printing Office, 1977).

Parkerson, Donald & Jo Ann Parkerson. *Transitions in American Education: A Social History of Teaching.* (New York, NY, Routledge, 2001).

Shipley, David O. *Neither Black nor White: The Whole Church for a Broken World.* (Waco, TX: Word Books, 1971).

Stentiford, Barry. *Tuskegee Airmen.* (Santa Barbara, CA: ABC-CLIO, 2012).

Thornton, Kevin and Dale Prentiss. *Building a Base: Selfridge and the Army.* (A TACOM History Office Publication, 1996). Accessed March 7, 2016. http://www.127wg.ang.af.mil/shared/media/document/AFD-140604-005.pdf

Tucker, Phillip Thomas. *Father of the Tuskegee Airmen: John C. Robinson.* (Dulles, VA: Potomac Books, Inc., 2012).

Veronico, Nicholas. *Hidden Warbirds II: More Epic Stories of Finding, Recovering and Rebuilding World War II's Lost Aircraft.* (Minneapolis, MN: Zenith Press, 2014).

Young, H. Peyton, *Equity in Theory and Practice*. (Princeton, NJ: Princeton University Press, 1994).

Zuchora-Walske, Christine. *The Tuskegee Airmen*. (Minneapolis, MN: Abdo Publishing, 2016).

ONLINE RESOURCES

1920 US Census, www.archives.com.
1930 US Census, www.archives.com.

Abandoned, Forgotten & Little Known Airfields in Europe. *Foggia Airfield Complex*. Accessed March 23, 2016. http://www.forgottenairfields.com/italy/apulia/foggia/foggia-airfield-complex-s561.html.

Ace Pilots. *Messerschmitt Bf 109*. Accessed March 22, 2106. http://acepilots.com/german/bf109.html.
Arlington National Cemetery. *Thomas Etholen Selfridge, First Lieutenant, United States Army*. Accessed March 2, 2016. http://www.arlingtoncemetery.net/thomaset.htm.

The Aviation History Online Museum. *Allison V-1710-USA*. Accessed March 3, 2016. *http://www.aviation-history.com/engines/allison.htmUnits*.

Ball, Jessica. *Mt. Vesuvius, Italy*. Accessed March 17, 2016. http://geology.com/volcanoes/vesuvius/.

Central Missouri Honor Flight. *About Central Missouri Honor Flight*. Accessed April 20, 2016. http://centralmissourihonorflight.com/about/.

Chivalette, William. *Corporal Eugene Jacques Bullard: First Black American Fighter Pilot*. Accessed March 7, 2016. http://www.airpower.maxwell.af.mil/apjinternational/apj-s/2005/3tri05/chivaletteeng.html

Co-Mo Electric Cooperative, Inc. Co-Mo History. Accessed April 8, 2016. http://www.co-mo.coop/co-mo-history/.

Dorr, Robert F. *P-51 Mustang's Switch to Merlin Engine Made it the World Beater of World War II.* (Appearing on Defense Media Network on October 26, 2012). Accessed March 24, 2016.
http://www.defensemedianetwork.com/stories/p-51-mustangs-switch-to-merlin-engine-made-it-the-world-beater-of-world-war-ii/.

The Flying Heritage Collection. *Focke-Wulf Fw 190 D-13 (DORA).* Accessed March 22, 2016.
http://www.flyingheritage.com/TemplatePlane.aspx?contentId=17.

Gathering of Eagles Foundation. Eagle Biography: Lieutenant Colonel Harry Stewart. Accessed March 23, 2016.
http://www.goefoundation.org/index.php/eagles/biographies/s/stewart-harry-t-jr/.

Haulman, Dr. Daniel L. *Tuskegee Airmen Chronology.* (Air Force Historical Research Agency, Expanded Edition: 23 December 2010). Accessed March 15, 2016.
http://www.tuskegee.edu/Uploads/files/About%20US/Airmen/TuskegeeAirmenChronology.pdf

Jackson County Government. *Biography of Harry T. Stewart, Jr.* Accessed March 23, 2016.
http://www.co.jackson.mi.us/Agencies/airport/docs/Stewart_Bio.pdf.

HistoryNet. *Curtiss P-40 Warhawk: One of World War II's Most Famous Fighters.* Accessed March 1, 2016. http://www.historynet.com/curtiss-p-40-warhawk-one-of-ww-iis-most-famous-fighters.htm

Jefferson Barracks Community Council. *History of Jefferson Barracks.* Accessed March 30, 2016. http://jbccstl.org.

Jim Crow Museum of Racist Memorabilia (Ferris State University). *What was Jim Crow?.* Accessed February 2, 2016.
http://www.ferris.edu/jimcrow/what.htm

Megura, Christie. *Missouri veterans connect future, past through Honor Flight.* Appearing in the August 26, 2013 edition of the *Columbia Missourian.* http://www.columbiamissourian.com/news/missouri-veterans-connect-future-past-through-honor-flight/article_af26cfef-54df-579b-84fe-670066d9f577.html.

Military Factory. *Bell P-39 Airacobra Fighter/Fighter-Bomber (1941).* Accessed March 22, 2016. http://www.militaryfactory.com/aircraft/detail.asp?aircraft_id=140.

Military Factory. *Republic P-47 Thunderbolt Fighter.* Accessed March 17, 2016. http://www.militaryfactory.com/aircraft/detail.asp?aircraft_id=76.

Miller County Museum and Historical Society. *Eldon Advertiser (date approximately 1966).* Accessed February 23, 2016. http://www.millercountymuseum.org/archives/081229.html

Missouri Department of Natural Resources. *National Register of Historic Places Registration Form: C.C. Hubbard School.* Accessed February 10, 2016. http://dnr.mo.gov/shpo/nps-nr/97000628.pdf

Missouri Digital Heritage. *Soldiers' Records: 1812-WWI.* Accessed March 17, 2016. http://s1.sos.mo.gov/records/archives/archivesdb/soldiers/default.aspx.

Mount Clements Public Library Local History Sketches. *The Founding of Selfridge Field.* Accessed March 2, 2016. http://www.mtclib.org/local%20history/selfridge%20field.pdf

National Archives. *Selective Service Records.* Accessed February 11, 2016. https://www.archives.gov/st-louis/archival-programs/other-records/selective-service.html

National Archives. *The Civil Rights Act of 1964 and the Equal Employment Opportunity Commission.* Accessed February 17, 2016. https://www.archives.gov/education/lessons/civil-rights-act/

The National Aviation Hall of Fame. *Charles Alfred "Chief" Anderson.* Accessed March 6, 2016. http://www.nationalaviation.org/z-anderson-charles-alfred/

The National Aviation Hall of Fame. *Charles Edward McGee.* Accessed March 29, 2016. http://www.nationalaviation.org/mcgee-charles-edward/.

National Park Service. *Legends of Tuskegee: Moton Field*. Accessed April 28, 2016. https://www.nps.gov/museum/exhibits/tuskegee/airmoton.htm.

National Park Service. *Tuskegee Airmen National Historic Site*. Accessed February 24, 2016. http://www.nps.gov/nr/travel/aviation/tus.htm

The National World War II Museum. *The Draft and WWII*. Accessed February 11, 2016. http://www.nationalww2museum.org/learn/education/for-students/ww2-history/take-a-closer-look/draft-registration-documents.html

Nebraska State Historical Society. *Lincoln Army Air Field, Lincoln Air Force Base*. Accessed February 26, 2016. http://www.nebraskahistory.org/publish/markers/texts/lincoln_army_air_field.htm.

Office of Missouri Governor Jay Nixon. *Gov. Nixon presents four Missouri veterans with Silver Star banners to honor their service and sacrifice*. Accessed April 25, 2016. https://governor.mo.gov/news/archive/gov-nixon-presents-four-missouri-veterans-silver-star-banners-honor-their-service-and.

The Official Homepage of the United States Army. *President, Congress Honor Tuskegee Airmen*. Accessed April 14, 2016. . http://www.army.mil/article/2476/President__Congress_Honor_Tuskegee_Airmen/.

Posner, Mary McCleary. *Salute to Veterans Celebration and Air Show: Our History*. Accessed April 19, 2016. http://www.salute.org/History2016.html.

Sheppard, James A. *Black Airmen In World War II*. Accessed March 17, 2016. http://www.bjmjr.net/ww2/black_airmen.htm.

Shipley, Galveston. *Centennial History of Prairie Grove Baptist Church*. Accessed February 23, 2016. http://www.moniteau.net/church/baptist/prairiegrove/prairiegrove.htm

Signature Aviation Matting. *A History of Landing Mats.* Accessed March 18, 2016. http://www.signatureaviationmatting.com/history-of-aviation-matting.php.

The Tuskegee National Historical Museum. *Who Were They?* Accessed March 18, 2016. http://www.tuskegeemuseum.org/who-were-they/.

Tuskegee University. *Tuskegee Airmen Pilot Listing.* Accessed April 12, 2016.
http://www.tuskegee.edu/about_us/legacy_of_fame/tuskegee_airmen/tuskegee_airmen_pilot_listing.aspx.

U.S. Air Force Biography. *General Benjamin Oliver Davis Jr.* Accessed February 16, 2016.
http://www.af.mil/AboutUs/Biographies/Display/tabid/225/Article/107298/general-benjamin-oliver-davis-jr.aspx

U.S. Air Force Biography. *General Carl A. Spaatz.* Accessed March 2, 2016.
http://www.af.mil/AboutUs/Biographies/Display/tabid/225/Article/105528/general-carl-a-spaatz.aspx

U.S. Army. *Army Aviation, Army Air Forces.* Accessed February 28, 2016. http://www.army.mil/aviation/airforces/

U.S. Army Center of Military History. *Naples-Foggia 1943 1944.* (A brochure prepared by Col. Kenneth V. Smith). Accessed May 1, 2016. http://www.history.army.mil/brochures/naples/72-17.htm.

WW2 USO. *United Service Organizations for National Defense Stateside Operations.* Accessed April 29, 2016. http://www.ww2uso.org/history.html.

INDEX

Roosevelt, Pres. Franklin D., 38

Ross, James D., 48-49, 64

Rudolph, Wilma, 101

Russell, Rosalind, 108

Safire, George, 28

Selfridge, Thomas Etholen, 59

Shipley, David O., 27, 106-107

Shipley, Douglas, 22

Shipley, Frances "Arvenia", 24-25

Shipley, Galveston, 20-21, 24-25, 31, 112-113

Shipley, Lee F., 107

Shipley, Leland, 108-109

Shipley, Kenneth, 117-118

Shipley, Mildred, 116-117, 119-120

Shipley, Timothy, 117, 119

Spaatz, Carl A., 60

Stewart, Jr., Lieutenant Colonel Harry T., 92-97

Taylor, Elmer W. , 78

Thomas, Etha D., 107

Tomhave, Colonel Jack P., 97-98, 129

Truman, President Harry S., 114

Turner, Andrew D., 77

Washington, Booker T., 45

Woods, Carroll S., 77